THE ANSWER KEY

Why is Teaching So Hard?

Al Colella, PhD

Joseph H. Crowley

Kimberly Deninger

The Answer Key: Why is Teaching So Hard?

Produced and printed by Stillwater River Publications.

Visit our website at **www.StillwaterPress.com**for more information.

First Stillwater River Publications Edition

ISBN: 978-1-963296-09-9 *(hardcover)*
ISBN: 978-1-963296-10-5 *(paperback)*

Library of Congress Control Number: 2024901087

1 2 3 4 5 6 7 8 9 10
Written by Al Colella, PhD,
Joseph H. Crowley & Kimberly Deninger.
Cover & interior book design by Matthew St. Jean.
Cover photograph by smolaw11 / Adobe Stock.
Published by Stillwater River Publications,
West Warwick, RI, USA.

Publisher's Cataloging-in-Publication
(Provided by Cassidy Cataloguing Services, Inc.)
Names: Deninger, Kimberly, author. |
Colella, Albert M., author. | Crowley, Joseph H., author.
Title: The answer key : why is teaching so hard? / Kimberly Deninger,
Al Colella, PhD, Joseph H. Crowley.
Description: First Stillwater River Publications edition. |
West Warwick, RI, USA : Stillwater River Publications, [2024]
Identifiers: ISBN: 978-1-963296-09-9 (hardcover) |
978-1-963296-10-5 (paperback) | LCCN: 2024901087
Subjects: LCSH: Teaching--Vocational guidance. | Education--
Vocational guidance. | Mentoring. | LCGFT: Self-help publications.
Classification: LCC: LB1775 .D46 2024 |
DDC: 371.10023--dc23

This book is for
the teachers who feel like
they are struggling.

This book is for
the administrators who want
to support their teachers.

This book is for
the parents who need to know
where to start.

This book is for
the students who rely on the system
to shape them.

The Book Trilogy: The Journey Continues…

Background (1995-2011): A faith-based ministry from a church in New England answers the call to the societal mandate to assist those in inner-city poverty areas across America. During these years, the 'journey to the inner-city of the South Bronx' developed into an outreach and community service ministry that received national attention as a model for similar action in other inner-city areas held ransom by poverty. More than 300 individuals made the journey from Rhode Island to the South Bronx , most multiple times. They bonded with the families-especially the children of this South Bronx neighborhood. During this iconic ministry-best described by 'the givers became receivers and the receivers became givers.' Significant life differences were made by each and all. However, the crucial question that emerged and rose to a crescendo was, "Why?" Specifically, why has such poverty-and its many inequalities-especially educational disabilities-persisted for decade after decade after decade…?

Book #1 (2010-2013): During these years, the moving recollection of a myriad of heart-warming and heart-breaking events and experiences provided a unique opportunity, basis, and motivation to capture the experiences of so many over this fifteen-year period. By all humanitarian measures, this became a 'rich' ministry! Book #1, *Let's Start with the Children* by Al Colella and Steven Lippincott, brought light and insight into *'Why is there so much sustained and increasing poverty?'* and *'What can be done?'* and *'If not now, when?'* This book is the motivation and genesis for its sequel [Book #2] in 2016.

Book #2 (2013-2016): *Poverty & Despair versus Education & Opportunity: Tearing Down Barriers & Building Bridges* by Joseph H. Crowley and Al Colella was published. This book addresses those questions cited in the previous paragraph. Poverty is characterized as a complex and convoluted arena, an organic and multi-dimensional entity that developed over many decades for a variety of flawed societal rationales. This festering situation has received many 'band-aids,' but sad as it may be, poverty and its impact on the quality of life, health, and opportunity of those living in poverty remains *unfair, undeserved, unnecessary, and unacceptable!*

Poverty-driven inequalities deny the impoverished those opportunities readily available to those residing beyond the virtual walls of poverty. Is education the response to poverty? The road out of poverty does go through the schoolhouse door, but this road is littered with so many poverty-driven inequalities.

Poverty & Despair versus Education & Opportunity has its companion website, www.poverty-inequalities.com, which was launched on 4/19/2016. This website is a recommended reference for Book #1 *and* Book #2.

Whereas Book #1 enabled the writing and publishing of Book #2, these two books forged the required Book #3 to complete the book trilogy to completely and factually tell the complete story of poverty and its terrible price to so many residing in poverty and its equally terrible litany of costs to so many millions—*especially the* children—for decade after decade…!

This trilogy—with the above-cited website—provides over 600+ relevant and supportive references for the readers!

Specific attention is paid to the poverty-education linkage/dynamics, which, historically, have prohibited millions of children for so many years from reaching the schoolhouse door. Additionally, for those children of poverty who do enter their schoolhouse, relatively few exit their schoolhouse with a 'meaningful' education. However, there is something that can be done to remove the litter from the road from poverty to the schoolhouse door. The authors—a teacher with eight years of experience in teaching primary grade classrooms and two professional and successful educators, each with more than forty years—have provided the experientially comprehensive model in Book #3 of this trilogy, *The Answer Key: Why Teachers Are Leaving* by Kim Deninger, Joseph H. Crowley, and Al Colella, published by Stillwater River Publications.

Their model provides the necessary and sufficient linkages to understand and pave the litter-free roads so necessary to reach, enter, and successfully exit their respective schoolhouses!

—Al Colella, PhD, Joseph H. Crowley & Kimberly Deninger

Authors' Biographies

JOSEPH H. CROWLEY: Teacher, Assistant Principal, Interim Superintendent of Schools, President and Executive Director of Rhode Island Association of School Principals, Chair of the Massachusetts Association of School Business Managers, Chair of New England Association of Schools & Colleges Commission on Technical and Career Institutions.

AL COLELLA, Ph.D.: BSEE 1961, MSEE 1965, Ph.D. 1973. Five years experience as a faculty member [all degrees through Ph.D.]. Thirty-three years with the Federal Government [technology, mathematics, systems analysis & synthesis, artificial intelligence, management & mentoring].

KIMBERLY DENINGER: Flagler College, Bachelor of Education (General & Special Education) with Certifications in English Language Learners, 2014; Masters: George Washington University, Masters of Education (Curriculum and Instruction) with Certifications in the Autism Spectrum, 2018; Masters Simmons College, Graduate Certificate (Applied Behavior Analysis), 2024.

In His Own Words: Joseph H. Crowley

IN HIS OWN WORDS, Dr. Colella focuses on the impact of poverty on the children who, through no fault of their own, suffer the many negative forces resulting from growing up in poverty. These children, born with all the potential of children born into more affluent families, often see that potential diminished by the stresses of living in poverty.

In my chance to offer a few words, I would like to reflect on the genesis of this book. Dr. Colella and I would often discuss the problems the author, Kim Deninger, encountered as she began her school teaching career. Dr. Colella was tough. He kept challenging me on what was wrong with the school systems. Why were children living in poverty falling behind wealthier children? Why was Kim having so much trouble with classroom management in her efforts to focus on learning?

Having five decades as an educator, I was inclined to side with the school systems. I knew first hand what growing up in poverty was like. I was familiar with the stresses of living in poverty. I had learned, with much reading, of the impact those stresses have on the brain development of children living in poverty. Learning gaps? Children growing up in poverty arrive at the school house door with learning gaps—long before schools have an influence on their learning. The conditions creating learning gaps before children enter school persist throughout a child's education. It is poverty that creates learning gaps—not schools. It is poverty that creates the behavior/impulse control issues, which almost led Kim to give up her dream of being a teacher.

Unfortunately, teacher education programs often provide little guidance in addressing the behavioral issues children living in poverty might exhibit. For the new teacher, classroom management seemingly becomes unmanageable. However, there are ways of relating to needy children that make the classroom a place of learning for all. That, in my view, is the focus of this book. There is no better reward for a teacher than seeing all of their students succeed. I would hope this book does just that.

—Joseph H. Crowley [BS, MBA]

In His Own Words: Al Colella, Ph.D.

THE 'MESSAGE' OF THIS BOOK is to address the children of poverty who do not receive the benefit of a meaningful education and, therefore, who do not have the opportunity to lead a productive life so readily available to those living beyond the walls of poverty!

That said, there are millions, e.g., twenty million children living in poverty in a given year. However, the population of children in poverty [many of whom become adults in poverty] has grown substantially over the years. This situation has a growing litany of costs beyond one's imagination!

Referring to the long-standing position of my colleague, Joseph H. Crowley, that despite the imperfections of some public school systems, 'schools are not the problem, the real and growing problem is *poverty!*' To emphasize his advocacy, let the readers recall those words—and belief—that "the road out of poverty goes through the schoolhouse door."

This book provides the readers with a rationale and accurate methodology to consider—and, most importantly, to understand—[1] the causes of poverty and its inequalities and [2] that a *national goal* for the reduction in poverty across America can lead to and enable the continuing reduction and elimination of poverty and its unacceptable and increasing spectrum of costs. As I stated in *Let's Start with the Children* nearly a decade ago, 'Poverty and its impact upon the quality of life of those living in poverty is *unfair, undeserved, unnecessary and unacceptable!*'"

—Al Colella, PhD

Contents

Authors' Biographies *ix*
In His Own Words: Joseph H. Crowley *xi*
In His Own Words: Al Colella, Ph.D. *xiii*

1. Letter to the Readers 1
2. Teacher Preparation 8
3. Are You Ready? 30
4. Learning Readiness 46
5. Poverty in the Classroom 60
6. Classroom Environments 78
7. Classroom Management & Teacher Leadership 88
8. Educational Model: Linkage & Dynamics 102
9. The Value of Mentoring for Children Living in Poverty 108
10. The Collective Poverty + Educational Costs 114

Epilogue 128
Chapter References 130
About the Authors 144

CHAPTER 1

Letter to the Readers

> The capacity to learn is a *gift*; the ability to learn is a *skill*; the willingness to learn is a *choice.*
>
> —BRIAN HERBERT

Kim's (Author) Opening Narrative: *'The Apple and the Tree'*

THIS NARRATIVE IS PROBABLY the most difficult and challenging narrative to write, but probably the most important. There are so many types of families, communities, cultural norms and expectations, and deep biases that it is going to be literally impossible for me to relate my experiences to the readers; however, I can share what I have seen and experienced in my early years of teaching and how that affects my practice teaching and the student's learning in my classrooms.

That said, every year, a new group of kiddos come into our classrooms with different economic levels, parenting styles, family dynamics, cultural priorities…the list goes on! But what can be counted on, in most cases, is that each kiddo is a reflection of their parents and their home and community environments . Perhaps more so in the primary grades; however, the theme is there. I am writing this through the lens that if a parent/family/guardians value and advocate the role of education, manners, respect, etc., then so will the kiddo! The same is true, in my experience, for the opposite point of view. If the parents, families, and guardians do not value those entities that shape the kiddos' lives and values that enable and promote positive behaviors in school, I regret to say that it will make the teachers' job that much more difficult, resulting in an educational and lasting disservice to the students. That is to say, it might not be impossible, but there will be one…maybe two… students in your career that you *can* help to foster behaviors separate from that of their parents/families/guardians influence and environments.

Story time: I had a student in my second year of teaching. I was teaching first grade in a charter school. I had a little girl who was all over the classroom. And I do mean 'all over the classroom': laying on the table, hanging off her chair, licking most surfaces…this list also goes on. She became one of my 'Elbow Friends,' meaning she needed to sit at my elbow all day to receive the prompting and proximity support needed to attempt to participate in the classroom activities and activities. As the readers may surmise, she was not making the progress for which I worked hard and hoped. I called home, i.e., single Mom and young babies at home, and asked if we could meet and talk about what has been happening in class . No meeting was set, and her telephone disconnected. However, the mother came up to the school during my lunch break to tell me that I, as a skinny white woman, was not going to tell her how to raise her child, and she left. I never called that Mom again, and I only did what I could for the student.

Fast forward to my fifth year of teaching. I was teaching 5th in a public school. I had a young boy who was going through his "I'm too cool for school" phase. He was receiving 'pull-out support' in math and was not participating to his full capability. After working with him in small groups and conferences, he was not changing his work habits, so I called his Mom at home [single Mom, two jobs] and asked if she could speak with him about his work habits and behavior in class. This mother came up to the school during *her* lunch and pulled him out of class to explain to him that 'school is his job,' and she should not have to stop her job because 'he wasn't doing his job...'

It was a great experience to partner with this Mom and get him to where he needed to be in math. "I became increasingly aware that *effective parenting* was a critical part of the education process [R 1-1, R 1-2]. If you have been in education for any length of time, you know that families can 'make or break' a student's success in the classroom. It is the family that forms the students' value of an education and helps them learn intangible skills—e.g., perseverance, effort, and grit—to keep trying even when the learning process is hard. It is also the community that influences and shapes the values of school and conduct. I'm writing this amid the recent Slap A Teacher Challenge on Tik Tok.

[R 1-3]. As educators, we cannot control what happens to our students before they come through our classroom door or what happens to/around them after school or during the summer breaks. Given that you will do your very best , it is *not* your fault if you cannot reach every single student—or even most of them or some of them during every school year. There were some years when I felt as if I was trying to go up the 'down staircase'; no matter how hard I tried or what classroom incentives I put in place, I could not convince a student to care/try in school. For a long time, I took that personally, so I wrote this narrative to tell the readers that "it's not your fault, it's not on you, you did everything you could and more!"

Teachers have to teach the students we have the best we can! If we are able to partner with the students' families to help foster and enable their role and investment in the educational process. I use the word 'investment' because not all students are going to love it, but the investment is in the long-term betterment of themselves and their futures as they move through their developments and out into the world!

My letter to each and every reader, teacher, teacher-to-be, Principal, and Administrator:

Dearest Reader,

My name is Kimberly Deninger, and I have just completed my eighth year as a teaching professional. During these eight years, I have had many (MANY) conversations with my grandfather, Papa Al. The late-night phone calls and early-morning emails to try and make my way through the year, the week, or even the day. I was desperate to understand why my simple desire to teach students was riddled with confusion and, sometimes, downright chaos. I shared my stories, specifically with my grandfather, "Pop," and his best friend. They have a heartfelt perspective of the overall education platform, so to speak, of the landscape of the education world. The inspiration and motivation for this book is to provide their insight on the connection between this landscape and the *very real* challenge of transitioning from a 'novice' or first-year teacher to a teacher who has the required skill set to bring 'teaching' readiness' into the classroom.

And it boiled down to this...My undergraduate years simply did not prepare me for the transition from learning how to teach to actually teaching. Teaching in my own classroom was, as it turns out, as straightforward as the school I attended or the schools in which I student taught. So then, what was it? Where was I going wrong? But let's back up for a second...

Year 1 (2014)—this is where it all began and one of the very first stories I shared with Pop and his best friend, Joe.

> When I sat down for my interview with the Principal and Dean of Students at the charter school in Jacksonville, it never occurred to me to ask about the types of learners that would step into my classroom, students that I would have a total of 180 days to teach and prepare for the next grade. I asked what now seems to be silly questions, such as what about reading centers? How important is staff collaboration here? I should have asked about the *preparedness* of the students coming into my room and the relationships the school had built with the commu-

nity and the children. In the initial weeks of my first teaching job, I quickly learned that neither of those things was in place. Out of my twenty-six kindergarteners, only two went to a form of Pre-K. While others may have been in care centers or with extended family members, the majority of my students started that September not knowing what letters looked like or how to sit down in a chair for more than a minute. I can assure you that teaching students to sit in a chair was not covered in my academic courses, at least not at my college, and I can guess that not at many others as well. At the end of the first week of school, I was panicking over how I was going to help these kiddos go from learning their name to reading a B-level book by the end of the school year! With no classroom aide, any day where none of my kids eloped from the classroom was a victory! All my well-organized lesson plans had not even seen the light of day. I can't even begin to count the number of tears I shed every day...Can I tell you that many tears were shed at the end of each day?

My teammates did their best to be supportive and help me where they could, but they were in similar situations as well. For the sake of sanity, there appeared to be an invisible rule at this school that teachers' main purpose is to get through to three or four kids academically and then establish behavior management for the rest. It broke my heart that that was the plumb line. How could that be the best for these kids? How could everything I had studied and hoped for "to make a difference" be irrelevant? It was a loud wake-up call that it would not be all "sunshine and rainbows," as it is most likely with any new job, but there was something bigger, something larger to grasp behind it all.

In this book, the larger landscape is laid out not to discourage any current or future teachers but simply to reassure you that you're not crazy. Teaching is hard and sacrificial. But you are needed more now than ever before!

To the best of my knowledge, current undergraduate educational/ teaching curricula don't sufficiently address the development of our 'teaching readiness' particularly when placed into a classroom environment where 'learning readiness' *should* exist but, in all too many cases, does not! And you have picked up or have been given this book because you feel the weight of that word, *should,* too.

The word *should* is often used when discussing The Hierarchy—my veteran teachers, you know exactly what I'm talking about. But let's catch everyone up so we all understand.

The Hierarchy—no, not Maslow's Hierarchy of Needs that we learned about in school but rather the hierarchy of national, state, county, and district to the individual school administration , the department lead, the teacher, and, THEN, the student. You might have seen some of the best educational goals and interests are lost or forgotten along the way of this hierarchy and, in some cases, some are replaced by something written by someone... in an office… who hasn't had a reading small group in years, if ever! You have heard, seen, and given a lot of things that *should* happen or what things *should* look like, but if you are or have ever been a teacher, I am sure you have joked with your teammates about having a District Representative take over your classroom for a day to see exactly what goes into a day in your room. You never truly know a person until you've walked a mile in their shoes. HA!

So the reality of all this "should" and why it's not is laid out in this sincere and well-researched book.

Hopefully, the following chapters and appendices in this book will help you see the connection between our perceived challenges in the classroom and what/who has the power to invoke change. That certainly is how I felt in many of my years, "Who's going to listen to me?" It is hard to be at the bottom of the pecking order when you're the first to be expected to fix something but also the first to be ignored. I hope this book will bring you clarity and some degree of sanity.

In the coming chapters, my grandfather, with the assistance of Joe Crawley, has written down what they have shared with me over the years. They have compiled the data, research, and diagrams they used to help me connect the dots, if you will, with why it was such a struggle those first several years.

> Learn to see. Realize that everything connects to everything else.
>
> —LEONARDI DA VINCI

See you on the other end!

Warmest regards,
Kimberly Deninger

CHAPTER 2

Teacher Preparation

> Improved education? Listen to the teachers.
>
> —BARBARA A. VONVILLAS [R 2-1]

Background

IN THE INTRODUCTION of this book, you are provided with chapter-by-chapter summaries. The genesis of this book and these chapters follows: after receiving my college degree for teaching in the educational arena in 2014, my first few years as a 'professional' teacher in the classroom were extremely challenging and even chaotic for my students as well as myself and my health! *As the author of this book, I would be irresponsible should I not share with its readers my initial realization that "I really was not prepared to teach!"* This initial and surprising realization was abundantly confirmed in my first several years as a teacher in the classroom! That said, this chapter addresses those additional *teacher preparation requirements* both within undergraduate and graduate programs and, especially, the early years in the classroom. Some necessary context follows: particular focus is upon the relationship between [1] the constantly growing student mix and diversity of classroom students and [2] its reality that has not yet been sufficiently integrated into those *teacher preparation* programs at the undergraduate level.

Most teacher preparation programs have, historically, been focused upon those primarily homogeneous student populations that have received the benefits of education from both established school programs with embedded mentoring and *continuity* of mentoring from their family, community, and social environments. Simply put, the majority of these students are *ready to learn*! It is important to note that their *learning readiness* is a lasting advantage and resource for their educational success. This particular student population, historically, matches well with the *teaching readiness* of their teachers.

Despite this historical 'success,' there were—*and are*—children who were/are 'left behind.' In recent years, there has been another growing population that does not have the advantage and resources of an equivalent education and learning environment. There is a constantly increasing population of students *unprepared* for the realities, challenges, opportunities, and responsibilities of school and social life and beyond. In the chapters ahead, you will discover that the greater majority of under-prepared children acquire *inherent disadvantages*! The advent of classrooms with 'diverse populations' only adds to the challenges for the *unprepared* teachers in these classrooms. Currently, this particular population also includes a steadily growing number of ESL [English as a Second Language], ELL [English Language Learners], TESOL [Teach English to Speakers of Other Languages], TEFL [Teach English Language as a Foreign Language], SEL [Social & Emotional Learning], and other students that are under-served in the area of *learning readiness.* Therefore, these children historically are not in sync with the *teaching readiness of their teachers.* Marks [R 2-2] provides an added and necessary insight into *teacher preparation requirements* for multilingual learners [MLLs].

To this point, schools across America are facing their most difficult staffing challenges in recent years at a crucial time when these student populations need *more diverse and effective teachers.* [R 2-3]

Teacher Preparation includes summaries of these on-point studies:

- *Perspective #1: of James A. Kadamus, the former Deputy Commissioner of Education in New York State*
- *Perspective #2: Ron Wolk, former Vice-President of Brown University*
- *Perspective #3: Sara Rimm-Kaufman, Commonwealth Professor of Education*
- *Ingredients of Teaching Readiness*
- *Issues that Compromise the Learning & Teaching Processes*
- *Educational Preparation for Teachers-to-be: Undergraduate and Graduate*
- *Understanding Teacher Shortages*
- *Diversity of Teacher Preparation Programs*
- *Role of 'Mentoring' in Education*
- *Some Reflections from New Teachers*
- *Resources for Teacher Readiness*
- *Common Sense Assessment [aka Reflective Preparation]*
- *Role of 'Behavioral' Analysis in the Classroom*

These thirteen cited areas are each related to *teacher preparation,* addressed in the following sections. These sections, individually and collectively, provide the necessary insight, foundation, and context for Chapter 3, *Teaching Readiness vs. Teaching Unreadiness,* Chapter 4, *Learning Readiness: Enablers vs. Detractors,* and, especially, *Teacher Preparation.*

Perspective of James A. Kadamus

James A. Kadamus is the former deputy commissioner of K-12 education in New York State. His consistent and preeminent educational experience and leadership become self-evident via his realistic and relevant articles.

This author has cited two of his articles:

> [1] Poor Teacher Preparation in R.I. [R 2-4]; this article is co-authored by Joseph P. Frey, formerly deputy commissioner of higher education in New York State, where he was responsible for overseeing teacher preparation programs. These two authors provide the following context: "*Whether the source of these teachers is the traditional teacher preparation programs at R.I. College, Brown University, and Providence College or alternative programs like Teach for America, the programs must demonstrate that they are also preparing prospective teachers to meet the challenges of working with* higher need students, *differentiate instruction based on individual student needs and understand how a student's culture and economic status impact how they learn.*"

These two authors also provide a set of very relevant and enlightening questions, e.g., [1] "During the clinical component of the [teacher preparation] program, do student teachers get opportunities to work with higher need students for enough time to hone their practice and assess their effectiveness?" [2] "Do college faculty continue to work with newly certified teachers once they secure a teaching job, or does their involvement end once they leave the teacher preparation programs?" [3] "Are faculty given credit toward tenure for working with teacher candidates and newly certified teachers in the classroom?" [4] "Are the knowledge and skills taught in the preparation programs aligned with criteria school administrators use to evaluate teachers in the classrooms?" [5] Do the teacher preparation programs use performance-based assessments that require prospective teachers to demonstrate effective teaching skills resulting in achievement gains for their students?" [6] "Are teacher candidates dropped from the program if they do not demonstrate an effective ability to teach?" [7] "Does the teacher preparation program teach their students how to engage parents and the community in supporting student learning and school improvement?" [8] "How are the programs preparing elementary teachers to provide effective instruction in math, science, and technology?" [9] "How many content courses in these subjects are student teachers required to teach?" [10] "Are they provided with appropriate project-based activities to engage students early in science, technology, engineering, and mathematics?"

[2] Five Key Steps to Fixing R.I.'s Schools, [R 2-5]; Kadamus refers to the Lawrence, MA, school system with a high percentage of Hispanic students, and students in poverty with conditions similar to Providence, R.I. He cites the five key components identified by Harvard University that are equally relevant for improving student learning in both Lawrence and Providence:

a. Create a culture of high expectations and aggressive performance goals.
b. Increase school-level autonomy as performance improves.
c. Improve the effectiveness of school and central office staff through a staff replacement system and a career ladder compensation system.
d. Expand learning time.
e. Increase the use of data for instructional improvement.

It is interesting to note that a collective effort by teachers, parents, community, and political support is necessary to understand, develop, and enable the inevitable tough educational decisions.

[2] Strategies to fix Providence's failing schools [R 2-6]; this Commentary dated 2020 serves to define the five-point scope of systemic effort required to enable a systemic educational success.

a. Implement a grade-by-grade curriculum across all elementary and middle schools to enable a consistent scope and sequence of content and skills for grades K-8.
b. Teach principals and teachers how to analyze and use state and local assessment data.
c. Create a robust professional development program that provides support for all teachers.

d. Set clear standards for student discipline and student and faculty attendance.
e. Create a team of mentors who work with the next generation of principals and other school leaders. *"The authors of this book would* readily add 'teachers' and 'families' to this team."

Perspective of Ron Wolk

R.I.'s chance to remake schools [R 2-7]; Ron Wolk is a former Vice-President of Brown University and creator and former editor of *Education Week*. In 2008, he received the Education Commission of the States' James Conant Award for his outstanding contribution to American education. Given the title of this article, the author provides his insight via his following statements:

- "It's time to depart from tradition."
- "Identify where the present [educational] systems are falling short."
- "Identify the leadership to make Rhode Island public schools among the best in the nation."
- "Identify and understand the current and required foundations [aka assumptions]."
- "The main problem is mainly [as in most states] is mainly one of performance."
- "It's clear that too many students are not meeting the standards set for them, too many teachers are not succeeding in getting their students to high levels of learning, and too many schools are poorly serving their students who either drop out of school or earn a diploma without acquiring the knowledge and skills they need."
- "Simply put, in 2015, we are relying on schools designed for 1915. And that isn't because we don't know what works today."

- "Before choosing the state's top education leader, the board of education has a rare opportunity (perhaps even an obligation) to re-imagine how public education can best serve students in the 21st century."
- "Change does not come easily-especially in education."
- Paraphrasing Ted Sizer: "The reason nothing important changes in education is because if one significant change is made, everything would have to change. And that is a scary prospect."

Two options immediately come to mind: [1] 'Re-imagine' and, then develop a systemic plan that would, in fact, enable those changes for *all* public school students. This first option is addressed in greater detail in Chapter 10, *Costs of Poverty.* Such a systemic plan requires *leadership, a 'temporary' additional budget 'investment' with an ROI that would effectively enable a 'reduction' in the constantly rising educational costs that address those schools that "are poorly serving a majority of their students who either drop out or earn a diploma without acquiring the knowledge and skills they need."* [R 2-8]. An example of this is [R 2-9] and its companion website https://www.poverty-inequalities.com.

Option [2] would be 'educational business as usual!'; e.g., *Providence Schools are Structured to Fail* [R 2-10]. The educational credentials of the author, Julia Steiny, speak for themselves.

Also, an added note from the opening quote from Teryn B. Clegg [R 2-11]: "Sometimes, as educators, we try to avoid, sidestep and minimize parent meetings. This year, I've tried to shift my perspective to *wanting* and *welcoming* parent meetings."

Kadamus also provides an earlier awareness with respect to the teacher preparation process and programs [R 2-12, R 2-13]. He also provides in [R 2-5] the following summary:

> The new teacher is never ready to teach on day one of their career. Like any other profession, a robust program of professional development and mentoring is necessary for them to be successful. However, the

professional development must build on an effective foundation of knowledge and skills a teacher receives in their preparation in order to become independent in the classroom. Asking new teachers to sink or swim without proper supervision, support, and feedback doesn't work.

It is in the best interest of all students in R.I. that the state promotes ongoing collaboration between schools and teacher preparation programs to keep the preparation of teachers strong and effective over time. Those teacher preparation programs that are proven to be successful need to be expanded, and those that are not should be disbanded.

Perspective of Sara Rimm-Kaufman

This author and well-documented educator/educational researcher is a Commonwealth Professor of Education at the School of Education and Human Development at the University of Virginia. [R 2-14]

Within the context of *the teacher preparation process*, the following are excerpts from [R 2-14]:

- Dr. Rimm-Kaufman's conducts research on elementary and middle school
- classrooms with the goal of using evidence to improve the quality of schooling experiences for teachers and students.
- The majority of efforts for creating excellent schools focus on curriculum, content knowledge, and accountability *and not the psychological experience and social interactions of students and teachers within them.*
- Her research considers the diversity present in schools [this author's note: "the constantly increasing diversity in magnitude and range!"], respects the challenges that teachers face every day, and recognizes the complexity of school improvement.
- In all her work, she has a steadfast commitment to *educational equity.*

Each of the cited four factors is relevant and necessary to the *teacher preparation process* and, collectively, contributes to the sufficiency of that process.

The author of this book [title of Kim's book to be entered here] certainly acknowledges, values the relevance, and endorses the cited individual and collective public school educational works of Kadamus, Frey , Rimm-Kaufman, and Wolk. Also, the author respectfully suggests they be integrated into future teacher preparation programs as required!

Additional Relevant Considerations [aka 'Food For Thought!']

One of the *very* necessary requirements for classroom success—for both the students and the teachers—is *effective classroom management strategies* that directly maximize the time available for the learning and teaching processes. There exists an abundance of singular teacher preparation courses throughout America's colleges, universities, and non-degree programs with specialized sets of courses universities.

There are also 'pieces' of classroom management topics that can be found within both undergraduate and graduate programs and courses. Some basic research has indicated that despite the proliferation of books, articles, papers, et al. addressing the topic of embedded classroom management. One might even ask, "Why aren't there more minors or concentrations for the teachers-to-be who might just find their inaugural teaching profession assignments in which classroom management is, historically, a significant issue, e.g., schools in areas of sustained poverty, that detracts from the educational processes for both students and teachers? This dynamic is addressed in greater detail in Chapter 7, *Classroom Management & Teacher Leadership*.

One may even ask why a significant percentage [36%] of teachers polled indicate that classroom management remains the dominant issue that motivates teachers to regret entering the teaching profession . A related question is what motivates the individual teacher to opt out of the teaching profession. Still another question: "Is there a nationwide teacher shortage, and is anything being done about it?"

Ingredients of Teacher Readiness

An integral part of *teacher readiness* is fully addressed in *Chapter 3, Teaching Readiness and Teacher Unreadiness:* in particular [R 3-8]. *For those public schools in which classroom management is a relatively minor consideration, i.e., the classroom time required for classroom management does not compromise the students' classroom readiness or the teachers' teaching readiness.* Conversely, there is an increasing number of public schools in which the time required for classroom management seriously degrades the students' learning readiness as well as the teachers' teaching readiness. The inevitable result is increasing compounding damage to the classroom educational process as the students migrate from grade to grade!

Issues That Compromise Learning and Teaching Readiness

It is critically important that the readers acknowledge and understand that *learning readiness, teaching readiness,* and *classroom management* are not independent or stand-alone entities. These three entities are dynamically linked and, therefore, must be considered together for classroom success for both the students *and the* teachers. Although *teaching readiness, learning readiness,* and *classroom management* are each addressed in Chapters 3, 4, and 7, Chapter 8 provides a *systemic* perspective of the functional educational model reflecting the linkage and dynamics amongst these three factors and others.

This perspective is recommended as the necessary foundation for the academic *Teacher Preparation* degree and related specialized non-degree programs.

Educational Preparation For Teachers-To-Be

Previous commentaries by Kadamus [R 2-4, R 2-5, R 2-6, R 2-12, R 2-13], Wolk [R 2-7] and Rimm-Kaufman [R 2-14] certainly frame the necessity to upgrade *Teacher Preparation* baccalaureate and graduate programs to keep pace with the ever-changing needs in public school education—in particular, in those schools with diverse student populations and those students living in geographical areas of poverty. Additionally, unacceptable teacher shortages have been increasing for several decades, giving rise to *a very crucial teacher preparation crisis* that impacts the entire public school educational system. As cited above, Chapter 8 addresses the impact of this growing teacher shortage crisis as it ripples through *each and all* of the functions of an educational *system.* It is acknowledged that the series of current and future viruses has been/is/may continue to be a contributing factor.

Unacceptable teacher shortages have been critically increasing for several decades; the critical impact on public school educational processes is also increasing! *Teacher Preparation—baccalaureate, graduate, specialized, and refresher*—programs currently face the need to keep pace with these growing classroom challenges, e.g., the changing needs of diverse student populations and unprepared-to-learn student populations.

Understanding Teacher Shortages

Not Enough Teachers [R 2-15] opens this reference with "An epidemic of teacher burnout has many school districts struggling to fill positions. Why are teachers unhappy?"

"How big is the problem?"

- In Houston, there were 900 teacher vacancies at the start of the 2022 school year.

- In Texas & rural Missouri, too few teachers cause a 4-day school week.
- In Florida, there are [about] 8000 teacher vacancies. Also, 450,000 kids started the 2022 school year without a permanent teacher.
- About 5,500 teachers quit in Maryland in 2022.
- Baltimore has 700 teacher vacancies.
- Kansas, Pennsylvania, Alabama, Mississippi, and Georgia have staffing crises in their classrooms.
- *Many of the nation's 3.1 million public school teachers have become deeply* disenchanted with the profession.
- Nearly ½ of the teachers polled say they intend to quit.
- 72% of school principals and school district leaders did not have enough applications for open teaching positions.
- Additionally, a 2018 University of Pennsylvania study reported that 44% of 'new teachers' resigned within the first five years of their careers. Five [of many!] relatively recent references are *4 Strategies To Increase Teacher Retention* [R 2-16], Understanding *Teacher Shortages* [R 2-17], *Are Teacher Shortages Worse Than We Thought?,* [R 2-18], *The Teacher Shortage Is Real, Large and Growing* R 2-19] and "It's Harder Than Ever" What We've Been Hearing About Teacher Shortages [R 2-20].

What districts are hardest hit?

Poor, rural, and urban districts primarily serving students of color. One report [of many] states that the shares of credentialed staying teachers are smaller in high-poverty schools. Another report offers that 'The teacher shortage is more acute in high-poverty schools,' e.g., the published estimates of the increasing shortage further underestimate the magnitude of the problem because the estimates don't reflect the fact that the shortage of qualified teachers is not spread evenly among all schools but is more acute in high-poverty schools.

Authors' reminder!

- A very recent article, *Kids Count Report: Teacher Shortage looms large in RI* [May 15, 2023; R 2-15a], provides an excellent overview: a summary follows:
- Within the mountain of statistics presented in Rhode Island Kids Count's nearly 200-page fact book, the organization's executive director, Paige Clausius-Parks, said she is "very concerned about how our children are faring during the continuing workforce crisis."
- For years, Kids Count, an educational advocacy group, has gathered, compiled, and released annual stats spotlighting weaknesses, disparities, and improvements in education.
- Rhode Island's educational challenges show that children are now being kept out of Head Start preschool programs because hiring and retaining teachers has diminished and low wages fail to attract enough [qualified] applicants.
- Rhode Island's educational challenges are not unique but local reflections of a national phenomenon. Across the country, "20% of Head Start and Early Head Start classrooms are closed, and there is an estimated waiting list of over 100,000 children," Kids Count said.
- Kids Count report also highlighted severe racial disparities that persist in many areas. Of the 15% of Rhode Island kids who lived in poverty from 2017 to 2021, 76% were of color.

Are there more long-term fixes?

- *Without major changes,* though, the pool of available teachers shall inevitably continue to shrink. [Author's note: Chapter 8 provides the much- needed *Functional Educational Model: Linkages & Dynamics,* and Chapter 10 addresses the '*total Costs of*

Poverty' and, most importantly, the candidate *opportunity* for a long-term fix!

Hanover Research [R 2-16] offers that 'teacher retention' has become a serious concern for many districts. This certainly reflects the national environment. For example, this report states that "facilitating their own children's learning has placed enormous stress on many teachers, leading some to decide against returning to the classroom entirely." This book provides a more expansive perspective on 'stress,' e.g., *classroom stress for the students and the teachers.*

These Four Strategies Can Help Schools Retain Their Best Teachers [R 2-21] recommends [a] Hold "stay" conversations with your strongest teachers, [b] Don't make teachers go it alone, [c] Survey teachers regularly, and [d] Celebrate great teaching.

Another report, *How a 30-Second Survey Can Help Schools Retain Teachers:* [R 2-22], poses the following question: 'Is a great resignation of teachers on the horizon?' Then, there is a TNTP Blog offering that 'There is no evidence of an uptick in teacher resignations so far this year ; an alarming number of teachers say they're thinking about quitting.' There is an abundance of evidence that there is a continuity of teacher resignations for more than a few years that has shaped the current *teacher shortage crisis* and its educational and damaging impact, which is addressed further in Chapter 8. *Are Teacher Shortages Worse Than We Thought?* [R 2-18] reports that—remarkably—other researchers have pushed back *against* the idea/evidence of a national teacher shortage. A Google search of *Teacher Shortages* yields a litany of reports that further address the many dimensions of 'the crisis of sustained teacher shortages.'

Authors' bottom line: "There is much work to be done in more than a few educational areas; certainly, teacher retention is a much-needed strategy. Perhaps it starts with the *teacher preparation* process!

Diversity of Teacher Preparation Programs

A reasonable starting point is a spectrum of 'best elementary teacher education programs' as exemplified by such programs at Michigan State University, the University of Michigan [Ann Arbor], the Teachers College, Columbia University, and more [R 2-23]. Another report [R 2-24] cites a spectrum of nine 'Teacher Education Programs in America' with categories & descriptions, e.g.., Program Length, Entry, Areas of Study, Special Features, etc.

It is also relevant that there are about 600 programs within the 'teacher preparation umbrella.' Related Google searches provide *preservice, alternative, special education, evaluation of, and perceptions* of teacher preparation programs.

"The main choice in most teacher education programs is between *elementary* or *secondary education.* However, within each, there exists a rather large number of possible majors and concentrations. Candidates studying *elementary education* can major in Talented and gifted student education, physical education, ESL, languages, art, math, music, science, reading, social science, second languages, theatre, and speech communication." Within *secondary education,* some universities divide their courses according to subjects rather than age group: for instance, you might be able to take your degree with a specialization in art or music education from pre-K to grade 12. Minors in education are also available for those who want to study education but don't want to go on to student teaching and certification. Colleges or Schools of Education also offer teacher licensure/certification programs for elementary and secondary education. This reference indicates that different states have different teacher licensure/certification programs. This can lead to graduate study in education.

Again, different graduate programs have different requirements. That said, this book can really serve as a '*Primer*' to assist teachers-to-be in selecting the candidate teacher preparation programs that best match their professional goals, teaching skills, and inner strengths!

Role of 'Mentoring' in Education

Mentoring is often considered as another form of '*tutoring.*' Tutoring is usually directed to a single 'student or several students for a specific academic and/or a much-needed academic and/or a social skill.' Mentoring is an expanded and multi-dimensional activity/function. That said, the primary role of a '*mentor*' can then be considered to be closely aligned to the function of a teacher in a specific *broad* area or *domain*, e.g., business, technology, medicine, health, military, sports & athletics, behavioral analysis, …, and, 'Yes!', even in the arena of education!

Consider the following:

[1] There was an engineering/technology faculty member at an outstanding university. He received an email fifty years after the graduation of one of his students. The student actually went to the same high school, but their paths had never merged. The student had never forgotten the engineering courses with this professor [Ph.D.] but, of equal importance, he also remembers a lot about life that enabled him to form a systems engineering company [fifty-four years ago!], became the CEO and retired to Australia, where he currently resides.

[2] Another student circa 1985 took engineering classes: his quotation, "In the Calculus classes with you, I recall that the tests were all open book and if we were stuck on a problem, we were to raise our hand. You'd walk over and take a look at what we were doing and maybe point to something on the page, underline a part, draw an arrow, or even jot down a quick formula to nudge us along or help us recall what we already knew. In other words, you used testing periods to *keep teaching! And I am here to tell you that it was a very effective method!....and what's really important is that your message was received, and I try to pay that forward, too, as I go!"*

[3] In the same spirit, in the same class, another student had failed Calculus not once but twice and was prepared to exit the engineering program. However, with guidance, encouragement, and *mentoring* from another professor, that student earned an 'A' and was also able to successfully earn the BSEE. What is the 'message' of these representative examples?

Mentoring is a very special teaching skill, for it unites the student and the teacher in a common educational journey. It is difficult to see documents with respect to *mentoring* in a curriculum or course outline because *mentoring* is really an intangible entity, i.e., it comes from within. *Mentoring, as addressed in Chapter 8, goes beyond the teachers and students!*

There are two references, [R 2-25] and [R 2-26], that are recommended . The title of the former, 'My Turn: Brave Teacher Gave Me Courage,' provides a very relevant *message*! The title of the latter is equally relevant: 'Fueling the Fire of Teaching Desire' and 'How tutoring is helping one future teacher.'

There exists, literally, an endless number of references and resources for teacher preparation, classroom readiness skills for both teachers and students, reflective teaching, and even those within the spectrum of Autism disorders!

Some Reflections From New Teachers

> *Beginning in Chapter 1 with my realization in my early years of teaching that "I really wasn't* prepared to teach*" in classrooms best characterized by students who were 'not ready to learn' and 'not supported by their families and community environment,' classroom management became the dominant activity by necessity...where I—and many other teachers—had little opportunity develop teaching skills and effectiveness. It wasn't pretty!*

Nearly two decades ago [2003], Mary Wilson Back wrote her thesis and dissertation based on her study of first-year teachers and their principals, addressing their perceptions of readiness among participants from traditional and non-traditional *teacher preparation programs.* Readiness competencies included Instructional Planning, Instructional Approaches, Learning Environment, Evaluation of Student Competency, Application of Technologies, Students as Learners, Professional Development, and Parent/Colleague Community Relations. The data gathered from 183 teachers and eighty-nine principals from three of the largest school districts in North Carolina indicated that principals' perceptions of readiness were less positive of new teachers than the perception that new teachers had of themselves.

An ambitious and interesting study that triggered some questions:

- What was the effectiveness of their *teacher preparation programs?*
- What was the level of advocacy, support, and mentoring provided by the principals or experienced teachers?
- Although five of the eight metrics were the basis for the principals of less positive perceptions, there were no significant differences among first-year teachers and perceptions of traditional and non-traditional *teacher preparation programs.* Could *this* conclusion provide some insight into the programs?

LEANLAB Education [R 2-27] offers a 'Teacher Sentiment Survey' gathering the range of sentiments from teachers. In this reference, student behavior was the most cited challenge for teachers; some teachers identified this problem as social-emotional health related to pandemic trauma, while others said that the problem's origin was the transition from a very unstructured virtual environment back to the traditional classroom model. Certainly, the existence and impact of the continuing pandemic are acknowledged; however, a more complete and useful model seems to be needed as a sound basis for meaningful conclusions.

Resources for New Teachers

As stated earlier, there exists a huge abundance of references/resources addressing the many components of the educational process within America's public school system. One purpose of these references/resources is to enhance *career readiness* and *employability skills* and, most importantly, students' and teachers' *classroom performance.* [R 2-28] offers the following:

- Every year, we hear the same challenge from hundreds of middle and high school teachers.
- The United States now has standards for workplace readiness education.
- But even though more schools offer *workplace readiness* courses than ever before, you [also] need lesson plans, projects, and other resources to teach *workplace* [aka classroom] *readiness.*

[R 2-28] provides the seven best resources to teach *workplace readiness* skills:

- United States Department of Labor
- Teachers Pay Teachers
- We Are Teachers
- California Career Resource Network
- Customer Service Blog Post from AES
- CareerOne Stop
- Workplace Readiness Curriculum from AES [Applied Educational Systems]

However, it's quite difficult to find *educational system* resources, e.g., protocols, strategies, skills, etc., that address meaningful models that provide relevant data/information for *meaningful functional models.*

These two points may also be helpful to the readers: [1] Each and all educational processes are composed of many components, and there are many resources that address some/many components...very many components. [2] However, although search engines provide an abundance of informative educational resources for components, there is a scarcity of information regarding *systemic* analyses of a specific network of certain components/functions and the network's linkages and dynamics. This latter point is addressed in greater detail in Chapter 8.

'Common Sense' Assessment [aka 'Reflective Preparation']

The basic form of 'common sense' assessment in *many, if not all, areas of endeavor is a two-step process!* Identify [a] 'What is *not* working?' and [b] 'What is working? The results of this basic reflection process enable the teacher to minimize [a] and maximize [b]. Also, this reflection directly enables improved effectiveness in learning, teaching, and classroom management.

Moving onto the *teacher preparation process,* there are resources available, e.g., teacher reflection strategies 'fueled by the teacher belief that all students can learn at a high level and that your performance as a teacher has a direct impact on student learning.' This reference provides thirty questions directly related to shaping the teaching skills and, therefore, the students' learning skills. The process of *reflective teaching* is also addressed by the British Journal of Educational Studies, an additional and valuable resource for valuable tools for *teacher preparation*:

https://scholar.google.com/scholar?q=teacher+preparation+journals&hl=en&as_sdt+0asvis+1&oi=schlart.

Behavioral Analysis in the Classroom

During the process of writing this book—especially my early and sometimes continued challenging and unpleasant classroom experiences [as provided in Chapters 1 and 6]—I became increasingly aware of my need to better understand the behaviors of some of my students. This awareness motivated me to take some courses in behavioral analysis to gain insight into and understand the many forms of the students' classroom behavior that directly interfere with classroom learning, teaching, and classroom management.

Internet searches for *behavior analysis-undergraduate-education courses* provided minimal data/information. For example, there are eight potential careers to consider for applied behavior analysis degree graduates.

- Market Research Analyst/Consumer Behavior Analyst
- Board Certified Behavior Analyst
- FBI Profiler/Analyst
- Human Resources Professional
- **School Counselor**
- **Special Education Teacher**
- Social Worker
- Researcher

Another interesting reference focuses on the constant growth of students with Autism Spectrum Disorder: 498 [1993-1994] to 31,1931 [2015-2016]. A growth of 529%! Board Certified Behavior Analysis reflects limited opportunities for undergraduates in teacher programs. However, it would not surprise the author if similar data exists for other learning-challenged students.

Currently, I find that taking select educationally related behavioral analysis courses is a useful resource and, perhaps, could be considered within undergraduate courses in teacher preparation. Finally, the reader is reminded that this book primarily addresses those students unready-to-learn for whatever the reasons may be.

Authors' Note: Some time and research were spent to properly address *Teacher Preparation* because of its relevance and necessity within the context of the book! Several years ago, Kim Deninger advocated that the topic of teacher preparation be addressed in Chapter 2 and beyond. Time has proven her right, as all the following Chapters 3-10 have their genesis and foundation in Chapter 2!

> So quickly does our childhood become ancient history that we forget to recognize the building blocks of our lives, our dedicated teachers. During the 1950s, these were usually unmarried women. For these women, their students became their family.
>
> —CHRIS FORTUNATO

> Although dated: "The essence and value of the above quote remain intact for the classroom 'family' environment to always include *all the students and all the teachers." No exceptions!*
>
> —KIMBERLY DENINGER

> Some books are to be tasted, others to be swallowed, and others to be chewed and digested. i.e., some books are to be read only in parts, others to be read, but not curiously, and others to be read wholly, and with diligence and attention.
>
> —FRANCIS BACON

CHAPTER 3

Are You Ready?

> Sometimes the thing your students need most right now has nothing to do with what's on the lesson plan!
>
> —ANONYMOUS
>
> The influence of a good teacher can never be erased!
>
> —ANONYMOUS

From: Kimberly

As we stand now, we know that there are two components we, as educators, must consider to be successful within our classrooms.

- Teachers must be well-versed in the curriculum being delivered.
- Teachers need to be able to adjust and pivot to meet student needs.

I am going to add a third:

- Students need to be ready to access, understand, and absorb what is being taught—*learning readiness.*

In my humble and experientially-based opinion, students are the most important members of the classroom. If they are not ready (prepared) to learn, then there is little I can teach. The above, Number 3, was what I was not ready for. I wrote earlier about how, when I stepped into my first classroom, I assumed that I would go right into the grade curriculum as I was trained for in my college program. I was quickly overwhelmed when students came into the room not knowing how to sit in a chair, what letters looked like or even the letters in their own name and other detractors [addressed in Chapter 4] ...and more.

Here is the crux of the problem. We are taught in our undergraduate programs how to teach a curriculum. I know I can comfortably go into any classroom and "teach." There are teachers who become very upset when they are evaluated and have less than sterling ratings. They know they were doing everything they were taught to be a good teacher. What the teacher education programs, in many instances, do not stress is everything happening in a classroom should be directed to learning. *An outstanding teacher presentation is worthless if students are not engaged with the learning that is supposed to happen as a result of the teaching.*

Let's start with the students this time. A great deal of what we are about to discuss is far beyond the control of your classroom. Bear with me.

> *Teaching readiness* is the necessary companion to *learning readiness.* Each is necessary for an effective educational process to exist; alone, neither is sufficient, but together, their synergism aligns with the three major factors for success noted at the beginning of the chapter. One other element, particularly in terms of new teachers, is an appropriate level of support and advocacy by the principal and administrative staff. We will endeavor to create a greater understanding of the four factors as readers progress through this book. A scan of the two references below will further enhance understanding of the focus of this book—children living in poverty have learning needs and learning readiness needs that go well beyond what the teacher is taught in a typical undergraduate teaching program:

A Framework for Understanding Poverty [R 3-1]
Poverty & Despair versus Education & Opportunity [R 3-2]

As I mentioned in my opening , I thought I was prepared to teach, but I was wrong! The impacts, individually and collectively, upon teaching readiness and student learning readiness [Chapter 4 and beyond] are [a] impaired impulse and behavior controls, [b] diminished concentration ability, and [c] impaired short-term memory.

I had not trained or studied for this. I remember sitting on the floor of my classroom, panicking over what I was doing wrong and how I was going to teach my students.

Teaching Readiness versus Teaching Unreadiness

Unprepared students are the students for whom the classroom must become a place to prosper. That said, let's look at the impact of the effective synergistic impact of *learning readiness* and *teaching readiness in* Figure 3-1.

There are a few things I would like teachers and teachers-to-be to consider using the Common Sense approach from Chapter 2:

- The goal to reduce, minimize & eliminate educational inequalities is achievable over time.
- If Goal 1 is achieved, the number of *unprepared* students will be minimized.
- Conversely, the number of *prepared* students will be maximized.
- The current negative educational inequalities will be lowered—teachers will be able to teach and students will be able to learn.

The impact of achieving the above goals is, ideally in the long-term, to enable all children to achieve a meaningful education so as to, in turn, achieve productive employment, upward mobility, income sta-

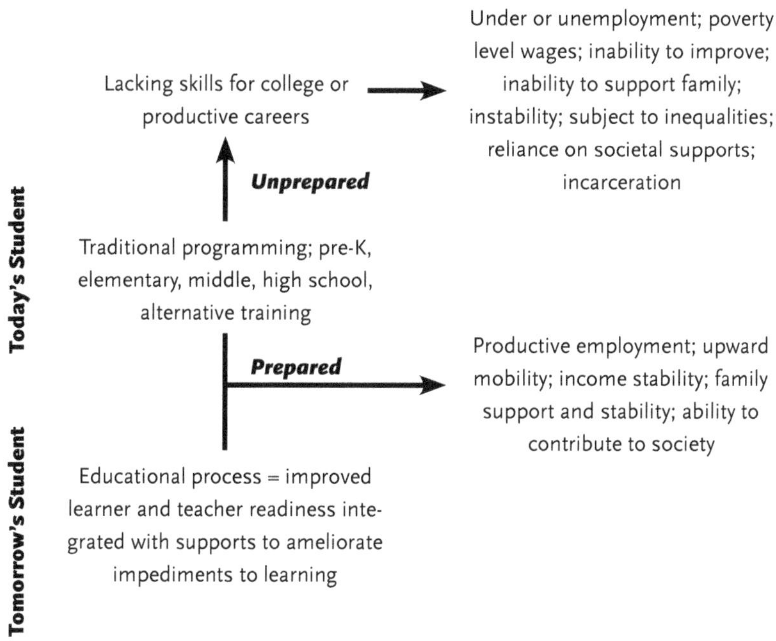

Figure 3-1. Updated Readiness Dynamics for the 'Prepared' and the 'Unprepared.' [R 3-2, p. 78]

bility, family and community support, advocacy and stability, increased health status, dramatically less incarceration, and, most importantly, the life-long inherent ability to become successful. In all, a most worthwhile goal.

Please note the above are educational system changes that *could, should, and can* be made. However, at the time of this book, they are just not our reality.

A more complete hierarchy of student readiness factors emphasizes the importance of learning readiness for the students but also, for us teachers, our teaching readiness requirements and preparation.

Readiness Model Components/Hierarchy

RF-1 Prenatal readiness [mother, child]
RF-2 Healthcare readiness [mother, child]
RF-3 Consistent family advocacy and support readiness [public & private sectors]
RF-4 Pre-K learning & readiness
RF-5 Grades K-3 learning & readiness
RF-6 Grades 4-8 learning & readiness
RF-7 Grades 9-12 learning & readiness
RF-8 Alternative education learning & readiness
RF-9 College teaching & learning readiness
RF-10 Life skills readiness
RF-11 Technology & literacy readiness
RF-12 Employment readiness
RF-13 Career/upward mobility readiness
RF-14 Societal participation/acceptance readiness
RF-15 Teaching readiness [throughout educational process]
RF-16 Advocacy & support [throughout RF-1, RF-2, ... RF-15]

Figure 3-2. Readiness model factors/hierarchy begins with the early years of family health and environment, the entire educational process, and the students' respective journeys of life. [R 3-2, p. 80]

First, Some Very Necessary Teaching Readiness Requirements

Included now is a meaningful and relevant quote that has been seen in numerous ways and on many different and colorful posters in our classrooms.

"One size does not fit all." [R 3-1, R 3-4, R 3-6, R 3-7]

This is a truism in all educational endeavors. One more time for the people in the back, "ONE SIZE DOES NOT FIT ALL!" If you have spent any significant amount of time in a classroom, you know this. I am sure that you, my fellow teachers, have been sitting in a Professional

Development or other meeting where this truism has been displayed and then followed up with more ways to standardize the learning or assessments in your classroom. Oh, the irony. Let's investigate it further for the First-Year teachers reading this.

It is fundamentally important for teachers (and administrators) to understand the creativity and initiatives needed to 'meet students where they are' so as to develop *learning readiness*. In the process, we also hone our *teaching readiness skills* to improve our effectiveness. Students are in different places on the educational ladder. It becomes our responsibility to provide the education and guidance needed to enable students to scale that ladder and become healthy adults and productive citizens.

The ladder of learning starts with the ladder set on a strong surface of teacher preparation. A preliminary rung is a student's readiness to learn. Upper rungs are unattainable if a child is not prepared, i.e. ready, to learn.

The Learning Ladder

EFFECTIVE LEARNING
Informative assessment
Teaching/learning style alignment
Positive school environment
Effective curriculum delivery
Age appropriate curriculum
Student's readiness to learn

The ladder must be supported by sound foundation of Teacher Readiness

Teaching Readiness [R3-9] offers the following question: "Has anyone stopped to wonder if student learning could happen without teaching readiness?" The author's perspective claims, "But very often the most crucial element, an undeniable prerequisite, and an uncontentious factor—

namely teacher readiness—gets overlooked in our discourses on approaches to maximize learning outcomes of our students."

The definition of teacher readiness needs to go beyond the pedagogical skills taught in most teacher education classes. Many students are more than capable of learning without the benefit of teaching. However, their ability to learn is enhanced by the ability of a teacher to *support* learning.

Ajtitha also provides guides that, collectively, provide a composite picture of what she means by *teacher readiness* [R3-9]!

- An uncluttered mind, ready to engage with the learning material in new ways.
- Openness to embrace multiple perspectives often impeded by rigidness and complacency that sets in because of mental conditioning over the years.
- Intrinsic motivation to learn and share the joy of learning by passing it on to others via teaching.
- Unobstructed progress on the learning curve.
- Thirst for self-discovery.
- Willingness to go the extra mile to maximize learning.
- Ability to transcend all obstacles and barriers in the pursuit of excellence.
- Preparedness to move out of the 'comfort zone' by taking untrodden paths of teaching to facilitate learning.

Lynch provides similar supportive strategies for *teaching readiness* [R 3-10]. Lynch also addresses the intangible linkage between *teachers' readiness* and *students' learning readiness!*

Another contributor to the enhancement of relevant teaching strategies and success is Rubin [R 3-11]. She identifies ten books enhancing the practice of teaching. Reference [R 3-12] cites 'soft skills,' i.e., communication, critical thinking and problem-solving, teamwork, life-long learning, information management, entrepreneurship, ethics, moral and professional skills, and leadership. These skills have a special resonance and relevance in Chapter 7: Classroom Leadership and Classroom Management.

An additional 'early-warning message' from *Tomorrow's Teachers* [R 3-13] by the Holmes Group of Michigan [Deans from major research institutions] cited the need to reform teacher education and the teaching profession. Some Holmes Group Notes follow:

- In addition, no teacher should be allowed to practice as an independent professional without at least a year of carefully supervised practice and advanced study in pedagogy.
- The undergraduate education for intending teachers is full of the bad teaching that litters American high schools.
- Successful reform requires the participation of both teachers and teacher educators.
- The 'One-Way Teaching' suggests that the responsibility for learning rests upon the students' shoulders and not those of the teachers.

So, how is it that so many newly educated college graduates often end up in their initial teaching assignments in low-performing schools? This is an interesting question.

When I was applying for my first teaching position right out of college, no one wanted me. No one wants the first year (twenty-one- year-old kid) and their lack of experience. I had to cast a *very* wide net to even get the interviews I did and was not confident when I signed that first contract. Let's remember that [1] most low-performing schools indicate unprepared students, and [2] relatively few undergraduate programs sufficiently prepare novice teachers for teaching assignments with unprepared students.

The term "low performing" is used because that is the label imposed on schools serving high numbers of children living under economic stress. There is much evidence this characterization is undeserved. A recent MIT study of Boston's busing students from "low-performing" inner- city schools to "high-performing" suburban schools is a fitting example. For fifty years, Boston has held a lottery for children in inner-city schools. Lottery winners were bused to neighboring districts for their schooling. The MIT study found no academic difference in the achievement between the "winners" of the lottery and those who were left behind in the inner-city schools. As noted previously, NCLB and its successor programs have done nothing to close the learning gaps between more and less affluent students by "fixing" schools because learning gaps do not originate, nor are they perpetuated by schools—it is about living under economic stress.

Beginning teachers often find themselves in under-resourced schools because that is more difficult than working with well-resourced schools. Between the stresses of working with unprepared children and few resources, many more experienced teachers find moving to a district with more resources provides a less stressful teaching environment. Most teacher openings, as a result, are in the poorly-resourced schools.

Some 21st Century Commentaries

- Joseph H. Crowley's 2015 *Poverty, Not Schools, To Blame For Low Scores* [R 3-14a] is exemplary. His continuing efforts—especially—for the children of poverty [currently around 20,000,000 nationwide] trace the debilitating impact of poverty upon their learning readiness and its lifelong duration. This outcome has directly shaped the challenge confronting the teachers in the classrooms of America.

- In 2016, this was followed by John J. Colby's *We Need To Teach Teachers Better* [R 3-15]. Colby poses the following question: "So how do education majors stack up against other students on the GREs? Sadly, they consistently obtain the lowest aggregate scores. Their bottom ranking tells us that, as a group, education majors are academically underachievers and, arguably, are not persons we want to teach our kids. It is interesting to also note that the Deans of the Holmes Group advocated more extended teacher training and higher achievement standards before a student could be awarded a teaching certificate.

- That said, Colby closes his incisive commentary with, "Teaching is a challenging profession that is complicated by myriad societal factors. Even with the best curriculum, schools cannot succeed unless teachers are inquisitive, broadly educated, and compassionate. We should insist that teachers acquire these attributes . Then, in addition to their success in the classroom, teachers should expect to be respected and compensated accordingly.

- In 2021, this was followed by Crowley's *OPINION, Making All Schoolchildren Winners* [R 3-14b].

- James A. Kadamus, formerly Deputy Commissioner of K-12 education in New York State, where he was responsible for overseeing teacher preparation programs. His *Poor Teacher Preparation in Rhode Island* [R 3-16] article poses six questions referencing *teacher preparation:*
    - Do college faculty continue to work with newly certified teachers once they secure a teaching position, or does the involvement end once they leave the teacher preparation program? Is there any feedback to assess the effectiveness of the teacher education programs?
    - Are the knowledge and skills taught in the preparation program aligned with the criteria school administrators use to evaluate teachers in the classroom?
    - Does the teacher preparation program use performance-based assessments that requires the prospective teacher to demonstrate effective teaching skills resulting in achievement gains for their students?

- Does the teacher preparation program teach students how to engage parents and the community in supporting student learning and school improvement?
- How are the programs preparing elementary teachers to provide effective instruction in math, science and technology?

Some of Kadamus's concluding comments:

- No new teacher is fully ready to teach on day one of their career.
- Asking new teachers to sink or swim without expert supervision, support, and feedback does not work.
- It is in the best interest of all students in Rhode Island that the State promotes ongoing collaboration between schools and teacher preparation programs to keep the preparation of teachers effective over time.

Authors' commentary: At this point, a responsible educational process addresses both the traditional populations of students and those *unprepared students of all ages* who are 'being left behind.' Certainly, no student should be left behind. The outstanding educational challenge, then, is to shape an educational process that, without question or controversy, leaves no one behind.

It is interesting to note that the learning and teaching readiness factors, when realized, could decrease the inequalities of Figure 3-3 [R 3-3, p. 82].

Simply put, deficiencies in learning/teaching readiness translate directly to increased costs past, present, and future and the lost *educational* opportunity to reduce the spectrum of costs over time. The costs of not educating children out of poverty—covered more in-depth in later chapters—are not limited to education. The inadequately educated student, leaving school, may need more in social service costs—unemployment, food and housing assistance, and medical care.

Definitions for Inequalities: INEQ-1 – INEQ-20

INEQ-1	Education
INEQ-2	Insufficient readiness
INEQ-3	Family, community & organizational advocacy & support
INEQ-4	Beyond academics [art, music, theater, etc.]
INEQ-5	Housing
INEQ-6	Access to medical care
INEQ-7	Health
INEQ-8	Life skills
INEQ-9	Employment
INEQ-10	Knowledge of and access to social services
INEQ-11	Transportation
INEQ-12	Upward mobility
INEQ-13	Justice system/access to legal counsel
INEQ-14	Income
INEQ-15	'Voice'
INEQ-16	Compassion/humanitarian perspective
INEQ-17	Domestic/street violence
INEQ-18	Adaptive strategies for those who fall 'through the cracks in floors' of the overall educational readiness factors
INEQ-19	Consistent and continuing accountability for the adaptive strategies of **INEQ-18**
INEQ-20	Overall quality of life

Teaching Readiness + Learning Readiness
= Educational opportunities enhancing the quality of life

Page 86 [R 3-2] was briefly mentioned earlier. That 'teaching readiness' was characterized as a necessary companion to 'learning readiness.' Each is individually necessary for an effective educational process, but neither alone is sufficient. Referencing Figure 3-1 again , the dichotomization of students into the prepared and the unprepared highlights that, for the most part, current pedagogical practices favor the prepared students. However, the dependence on learning and teaching readiness disadvantages the unprepared students. These include those growing student populations where the axiom 'one size doesn't fit all' applies most, leading to school drop-outs with a lack of real-world skills and unemployment.

Educational Improvement

There is a perspective offered by a Special-Needs Administrator who has successfully developed programs to teach teachers how to teach. This entails both the tangible, e.g., words and techniques, and those intangible entities, e.g., spirit, encouragement, and a 'can-do' mind-set [R 3-8].

It is both interesting and enlightening that these qualities 'come from within,' i.e., the mind, heart, and spirit!

Learning	*Imagination*
Authority	*Compassion*
Ethics	*Patience*
Order	*Character*
Pleasure	

I would add *empathy* and *the gift of encouragement* that great teachers pass on to their students, enabling them to develop the self-belief, will, and energy that can be successful in the classroom and life.

This can be taken to mean it is not so much what you teach but how you teach; meeting the needs of students where they are and providing them the guidance and support needed to grow as learners and to achieve success in their own way.

Two additional recommendations:

[1] **OPINION/Crowley: Making all schoolchildren winners, Providence Journal, February 7, 2021** [Author Joseph H. Crowley's excerpts [R 3-14a] and an earlier, by six years, 'alerting perspective' [R 3-14b]:

- Many believe our high-poverty schools are "failing" without understanding what the label failing is based on.
- A "failing school" is one that does not close [learning] gaps.
- This term does not mean the school is *failing* in any broader sense. There needs to be a distinction between stating a school has learning gaps versus saying a school is failing.
- Charging schools with learning gaps would make sense if learning gaps were created by schools.
- The National Assessment of Educational Progress has verified that twenty years of NCLB and billions of dollars spent on "fixing" failing schools have been an utter failure, i.e., the learning gaps have not closed—at all.
- Why? Because learning gaps do not come from schools. *Learning gaps come from living in the various strata of poverty.*

[2] **Kimberly's suggested helpful references:**

1. TNTP *{insight@tntp.org}*: TNTP Learning Experience Survey for School Year 2020-2021. Survey results for students with school and/or grade categories, learning method, wellness, access, connectedness and support, student learning, communication, and expectations. Same categories for parents/guardians.
2. *A study of first-year teachers and their principals: Perceptions of readiness among participants from traditional and non-traditional teacher preparation programs.*
3. *Embedding soft skills to the teacher undergraduate curriculum: perception of faculty and students. Vithariapathirana* [11/18/20].
4. *7 Best Resources to Teach Workplace Readiness Skills* [Career Readiness/Employability Skills], Bri Stauffer [11/26/2017].
5. *K-12 Blended Teaching Readiness: Model and Instrument Development, Charles R. Graham, Jered Borup, Emily Pulham*

& Ross Larsen, Journal of Research on Technology in Education, Volume 51, 2019, pp. 239-58.

6. Novice Teacher Perceptions of the Soft Skills Needed in Today's Workplace, Tang Keow, Nor Hashimah Hashim, Hashimah Mohd Yunus, Global Conference on Contemporary Issues in Education, GLOGE-EDU, pp. 12-14, 2014, Las Vegas, USA.

I've learned that people will forget what you said...
people will forget what you did...
but people will never forget how you made them feel!

—MAYA ANGELOU

If you are not willing to learn, no one can help you.
If you are determined to learn, no one can stop you.

—ZIG ZIGLAR

More from Kimberly and her two co-authors [Al Colella and Joe Crowley]: Looking ahead—recommendation for the readers beyond this Chapter.

We hope this guidance can be called 'connecting the dots'—a process that enables readers to have a wider vision and a greater understanding of any process, activity, or effort in any area of endeavor. Learning and teaching readiness are two subsystems within the larger system of public education. Both learning and teaching readiness can be further divided into more subsystems. As an example, the classroom environment is a subsystem of the teacher readiness subsystem.

Using the connection between learning readiness and teaching readiness as parts of the education system model, the forthcoming chapters are the building blocks, or subsystems if you will, leading to Chapter 8 [Systemic/Inclusive Educational Model]. Chapter 8 seeks to tie the previous chapter subsystems into a whole.

Chapter 9 [Roles of Advocacy, Support & Mentoring for the Classroom Teachers] provides another 'dot' that is an integral component for the schools' educational process to be successful for the teachers and student populations in need.

Chapter 10 [COLLECTIVE EDUCATIONAL COSTS] addresses that spectrum of costs beyond the traditionary educational costs. A lack of understanding of the costs related to perpetuating poverty by not providing students the educational wherewithal to rise out of poverty limits the political will to provide the resources to accomplish that mission. As the old auto mechanic ad once said, "You can pay me now or pay me later." The costs incurred by paying later, as is a general rule, far exceed the costs of making appropriate educational investments now. The general lack of understanding of the costs of poverty is a major factor in not addressing those costs.

The three authors would certainly be irresponsible should they not provide acknowledgment, commendation, and gratitude to all those teachers who have enabled classroom success and shaped the lives of millions of students. The same is offered to all those millions of students and teachers who have struggled to overcome the handicaps of *teaching unreadiness* and *learning unreadiness.*

CHAPTER 4

Learning Readiness

> The beautiful thing about learning is that nobody can take it away from you.
>
> —B.B. KING

READINESS, AKA PREPAREDNESS, is a crucial and necessary ingredient for success in any endeavor, e.g., the business world, politics, sports, military operations, medical practices, and, especially, the educational arena at all levels. There are no substitutes or shortcuts. Conversely, the lack of readiness is likely to result in, if not failure then, less than optimal results.

A simplistic example of readiness. You have your favorite coffee travel cup. You are ready to fill it but its cap is on—much like you are prepared to fill your students' heads with knowledge. You do your best to pour, which results in a mess. If you do not remove the cap on your carry cup, your cup is not ready to hold your coffee much like your students. If you cannot remove the "cap" on your students' learning readiness, you can "pour" all the knowledge you want. If your students are not ready to learn, no matter how good a teacher you are, no learning is likely to take place. That is the essence of this book: Addressing the caps on learning readiness.

It might be helpful to review *Determinants of Learning* [R 4-1], which provides a breakdown of learning readiness factors, i.e., physical, emotional, experiential, and knowledge readiness. In turn, each of these is further defined, e.g., the four factors of knowledge readiness are one's knowledge base, cognitive ability, learning disabilities, and learning styles—each of which is directly relevant to classroom performance within the context of this chapter.

There has always existed the need to improve the effectiveness of America's public schools' educational systems. Chapter 3 provided some necessary insight into such well-intended attempts, e.g., the Common Core curriculum, standardized testing and those national programs, e.g., America 2000 [President Bush, Sr.], Goals 2000 [President Clinton], the Common Core Curriculum, standardized testing, and other national programs, e.g., No Child Left Behind [NCLB, President Bush, Jr.] and Race To The Top [RTTT, President Obama]. Chapter 3 also recalls the common belief that schools created 'learning gaps' rather than eradicating a poverty environment. Lost were the many years of opportunity and billions of dollars that could have been directed to addressing the real issue, i.e., living in a poverty environment with minimal learning support and its companion outcome of continuing educational disadvantages and disabilities.

The system of' social promotions' allowed children to be promoted from one grade level to the next despite their lack *of learning readiness* and academic foundation to meet the requirements for promotion [R 4-2]. Unfortunately for the students and the teachers who were responsible with integrating the students into their classes, no efforts were made between June and September to address the lack of readiness issues, most likely to become problematic during the next school year.

Research has reflected the high drop-out rates for students retained in grade. Retention has myriad detrimental impacts on students. Watching one's peers move ahead and then being placed in a class with younger children is a slam to one's self-esteem. Children who are retained have identifiable deficits in their learning, which may impact their ability to grasp more advanced concepts. However, it is not that they did not learn anything. To make them repeat everything because 'they didn't get something' does not make sense. The most logical—and most economical—solution would be to identify and address the deficits so that the student can progress with his or her peers. *An effective means of addressing these deficits is provided in a forthcoming chapter!* The term 'economical' refers to the added cost of a school year to that child's education. To pay that cost only to see the child ultimately drop out of school is senseless. The extended school day and school year proposed as a remedy for closing learning gaps would provide the opportunity for assessing students' needs and addressing any learning readiness deficits.

Learning Readiness in the Classroom

With some exceptions, most children who live beyond the walls of poverty, by and large, have an acceptable or better 'readiness to learn' by virtue of the quality of their education prior to entering school. Keeping in mind the dual reality of children in poverty and those who are not, the question then becomes, «What is the status of readiness for the children of sustained poverty as they enter the pre-K, K, grades 1, 2,...?" This book provides an eye-opening view of the classroom behaviors and environments that result from the lack of readiness of these unprepared students. There exists little opportunity to successfully counter their lack of readiness until such lack becomes apparent in the classroom. Only then is it possible to address the lack of learning readiness issue, but alas, few teacher training programs provide aspiring teachers with the tools to address the issue. Lack of readiness—aka unreadiness—poses a continuing serious disadvantage to the child's ability to acquire a meaningful education and a serious issue for classroom management, as stated in Chapter 3. As Crowley [*Poverty, not schools, to blame for low scores* [R 4-3]] offered on November 27, 2015. Also—and simply put—Colella and Lippincott [*Let's Start with the Children,* 2013 [R 4-4]]: "Remember that father from the South Bronx who offered that living in the poverty of the South Bronx is like living in a dark room and not knowing how to get out and, then, there is no one to show him the way." That 'dark room' is residence in sustained poverty! It is also an indicator of the outstanding challenge—addressing the issue of learning 'unreadiness.'

Poverty/Education Connection

Many of us can remember studying that the odds of being poor are greatly increased if you are a child born into poverty. The road out of poverty is a *meaningful* education. The greatest roadblock to a good education is to be born into poverty.

'Poor,' being of low socio-economic status [SES], is a complex condition. There are urban, suburban, and rural poor, all manifesting their poverty in slightly different ways. There is *situational* poverty, which may occur through a job loss, illness, divorce, or other similar setbacks of life—especially difficult and an added burden for those already living in poverty or marginally so. There is *generational* poverty, which becomes a way of life, an organic, cyclic culture, in which individuals and families learn survival by dependence on the system of governmental and private support programs and even families. Yet, as diverse as poverty is, it produces strikingly similar symptoms, one of which is a negative impact on a child's ability to be successful in the classroom.

Regardless of the type of poverty, living in sustained poverty creates stresses in number, intensity, frequency, and duration not typical in middle or upper-class families [although middle-class families transitioning to marginal and beyond are increasing [R 4-5], [R 4-6]. There are two factors differentiating students. First, the stresses of living in poverty create cortisol. Cortisol, in turn, when produced over a sustained period of time, creates brain challenges, leading to impaired behavior control, short-term memory, and concentration. Secondly, when the home environment is not able to provide access to early learning building blocks, a gap forms. As an example, take two children. One has been exposed to the ABC song since they were two years old. The other child has never been exposed to the ABCs in any shape or form.

Walking through the schoolhouse door, which child is going to be considered 'learning ready'?

There are several indicators in Chapter 3 that reflect/indicate that there exist two distinct student populations, currently 'those living in poverty and those who do not' [R 4-7]. However, the opportunity of an extended school day and school year enables a significant reduction in learning gaps. A supportive multi-dimensional mentoring program, i.e., academic, social skills, life skills, 'can do' environment et al. [Chapter 8] offers an added reduction. Although cortisol impacts learning to a degree, the more educationally rich environment of homes with economic advantage gives these students more 'out-of-school' education and education supports than those available to children living in poverty. However, research at Johns Hopkins University indicated that children in poverty learned at about the same level as their peers outside the poverty level in school [assuming that there is a reasonable/acceptable level of classroom management!]. Non-poverty children moved ahead, at least in standardized test scores, during the summer when schools were closed. The difference was in the regression rates between the not poor and the poor. Children, living in poverty, fell back far more. The economically challenged children do not do as well on standardized tests because of what may not be available in their homes.

From Education Week, *Standards-Based Accountability's High Stakes* [https://www.edweek.org/ew/articles/2011//11/03/09/23wolk_ep.h30.html [R 4-8]] offers four indisputable facts that capture the essence of America's educational system's failures:

- The National Assessment of Educational Progress [NAEP] reports that only three of ten seniors score 'proficient' in reading, writing, math, and science on average. Scores generally decline from the 4th to 12th grade.
- Of the one hundred students who start the 3rd grade, about one-third drop out, and another third graduate not adequately 'ready' for college or the workplace.

- The NAEP data is an indictment of the entire American public school education system. This astonishing failure falls primarily on *poor* and *minority children*, who are literally trapped on the wrong side of the learning and achievement gaps.
- During a decade of No Child Left behind [NCLB] and Race To The Top [RTTT], the NAEP scores did increase. Literacy and math scores increased by an average of ten points over ten years, increasing from 240 to 250 on a 500-point scale. It has already been mentioned about the billions of dollars spent on this dismal improvement. However, the twenty-point gap between lower and upper SES students on average remained unchanged. To belabor the point, the goal of both NCLB and RTTT was to eliminate this gap.

That said, this book shows the chain reaction of [1] children's residence in sustained poverty, [2] poverty-enabled stresses, [3] the impact of these sustained stresses upon the learning readiness and social behavior of these children, especially within a classroom setting, [4] the resultant extraordinary requirements for classroom management and [5] the inadequacies of classroom management skills related to working with children from poverty environments, [6] the resultant educational and humanitarian costs for the children of poverty and finally, [7] the steadily increasing national, state and local budgetary costs.

Brain impairment is a direct consequence of children being exposed to many stresses for an extended duration. The children begin life with the same potential as other children. Although they may begin life with the same potential, the impact of the poverty-environment in which they live interferes *with their ability to learn* and *to acquire the necessary behavioral skills to behave appropriately in classroom settings* and to be as successful as children not plagued by the stresses of poverty.

Why this is so is well documented through hundreds of research studies. Research points to two intertwined conditions. Living in poverty provides little of the support and advocacy for education found in non-poverty homes—the educationally impoverished home environment is a debilitating arena. And, the resultant stresses of living interfere with brain development in ways critical to learning [R 4-9], [R 4-10], [R 4-11], and [R 4-12]. Education can play a crucial role in preparing these children for productive roles while also emphasizing that the schools cannot, by themselves and with their current increasingly limited resources, undo all of the impediments to learning triggered by growing up in poverty.

Many of us in the classroom have seen the impact of poverty on education—specifically, the unreadiness of our students to learn' and a lack of necessary social and classroom behavior skills. Behavior is a critical factor in creating an educationally productive classroom. We often hear of teachers lamenting that they spend their days in classroom management while little learning goes on. Pre-school for all children living in poverty provides an opportunity for addressing behavioral issues prior to kindergarten. Summer programs between pre-K and K provide more of a nurturing environment known to be an antidote to the toxic effects of stress-induced cortisol—cortisol overdoses, being the genesis of the lack of behavioral controls. Minimizing the impacts of cortisol-created brain issues will have long-term benefits, not the least of which are reduced teen pregnancies, poor health habits, and drug and alcohol abuse [R 4-13].

Finally, there is one point upon which there is little argument. America would be a better and safer place if it was clearly understood—*and practiced*—that our children—*all our children*—are a national resource to be developed.

According to a 2009 McKinsey report, The Economic Impact of the Achievement Gap in America's Schools, America would also be wealthier, with the Gross Domestic Product increasing by 3% to 5% as learning gaps closed [R 4-14]. Additionally, it would be both sad and irresponsible if the loss of opportunity for so many children is left unacknowledged.

Poverty Induced Stressors:

- Inadequate nutrition
- Food uncertainty
- Housing uncertainty and instability
- Poor quality of life
- Single parenthood
- Minimally educated parents
- Lack of more suitable role models
- Parent absenteeism (including parent incarceration)
- Health issues
- Broken homes
- Inadequate income
- Legal inequality
- Justice inequality
- Mainstream separation
- Poor poverty-influenced choices
- Lack of advocacy
- Incarceration/Recidivism
- Devalued education
- Domestic violence/abuse
- Poor parenting practices [harsh parenting]
- Parents with alcohol/drug issues
- Parents with mental health issues
- Street violence
- Little upward mobility
- Gang affiliation/influences
- Discrimination
- Prejudice
- Depression
- Inadequate child care, e.g., television/technology as a babysitter

Outcome of Stressors

As noted in the above litany of *poverty-induced stresses*, the two most negative forces coming into play are [1] the stresses of living in a poverty environment and [2] the conditions of the children that separate them from their non-poverty peers. The outcome of any combination of these stresses are {1} impaired brain development and {2} the inability for the individual to control behavior issues, impaired short-term memory and concentration, which, left unabated, may last a lifetime, attention deficit limitations often lasting life-long.

The outcome of an environment of poverty is a smaller vocabulary, fewer literacy and math skills, suffering more social and emotional issues, having less access to cultural enrichment and athletic activities, little interaction with family and community mentors, suffering from more malnutrition and untreated medical and dental conditions and having less access to the reading material and technology so readily available to those children living beyond poverty.

Brain research has established that cortisol, the stress chemical released as a result of multiple and long-term stressors, impairs a child's ability to make sound behavioral judgments, creates 'pay attention' issues, and impedes their short-term memory. These are the factors creating a lack of readiness to learn and, as many of us have found, lead to classroom disruptions impacting the classroom as a whole. Although representing a minority [about 20%] of the population of school children, they represent the vast majority of students being retained in grade, are more often disciplined, exhibit learning gaps in standardized test scores, and graduate at a far lower rate.

For example, Joan Luby, Professor of Psychiatry at the Washington School of Medicine in St. Louis, published the results of a study on 145 children in JAMA Pediatrics [R 4-15]. Luby's report mirrors previous research done at McGill University [R 4-16] and *The Adverse Childhood Experiences* [R 4-17]. Essentially, Luby's findings concluded that stresses release cortisol, leading to brain changes resulting in hyperactivity and attention deficits. The JAMA Pediatrics abstract states, "Findings substantiate the behavioral literature on negative effects of poverty on child development and provide new data confirming that effects extend to brain development."

A Mayo Clinic article, *Chronic Stress Puts Your Health at Risk* [R4-18], offers some observations about "When the natural stress response goes wild." Specifically, when stressors are always present [as in a sustained poverty environment], and one constantly feels under attack, the previously mentioned fight-or-flight reaction stays on. The long-term activation of the stress-response system and the overexposure to cortisol and other stress hormones that follow can disrupt almost all of a body's processes, i.e., increased risk of many health problems, so very common in areas of poverty, including:

- Anxiety
- Depression
- Digestive problems
- Headaches
- Heart disease
- Sleep problems
- Weight gain
- Memory and concentration impairment
- The inflammation throughout one's body created by cortisol is a factor in myriad physical ailments [cancers, heart issues, etc.] and mental health issues throughout one's lifetime.

The Mayo Clinic provides a list of stress management strategies. As the readers look through the list and bring to mind some of the neediest students, it becomes readily apparent that this list is for those who can afford the cost of these strategies. Conversely, it is not a list with any meaning for those children in economically challenging environments addressed earlier in this chapter and Chapter 3.

- Eating a healthy diet, getting regular exercise, and plenty of sleep
- Practicing relaxation techniques such as trying yoga, practicing deep breathing, getting a massage, or learning to meditate
- Taking time for hobbies, such as reading a book or listening to music
- Fostering healthy relationships
- Having a sense of humor
- Volunteering in your community
- Seeking professional counseling when needed

Of critical importance for educators [and educators-to-be], myriad research reports indicate nurturing is an antidote to chronic cortisol exposure. The nurturing classroom is the best chance for children to escape the brain damage caused by cortisol. Ironically, and unfortunately, the misbehaving or non-attentive child may be less likely to be nurtured but rather be punished for misbehaving and being non-attentive.

This research-based outcome translates directly to trying times and challenges for the administrators, teachers, and, most importantly, the children—and their families. For example, No Child Left Behind [NCLB] created the misconception that the learning gaps between the children of poverty and those non-poverty children were a problem created by the schools. Disciplinarians, unfortunately, accepted the notion that misbehavior is always a willful act, requiring some form of punishment. However, research studies have proven that home environments create learning gaps, and much misbehavior is largely due to one cause—cortisol [R 4-17].

Psychology Today [R 4-19] has described cortisol as Public Enemy Number One as it "wreaks havoc on one's mind and body." The damage is most severe for adolescents. MIT News has reported that high exposure to poverty-induced stressors leads to brain changes correlated to standardized test scores.

That said, it becomes appropriate to clearly acknowledge and understand the 'chain reaction' between poverty, poverty-induced stressors, stressor-enabled cortisol levels, hyperactivity, attention deficits, and classroom behavior [R 4-18]: what we are defining as 'learning unreadiness.' However, there are more elements that manifest themselves in so many classrooms serving the children of poverty. Simply put, 'learning unreadiness' is an outcome of growing up in an environment dominated by poverty. The ultimate antidote for 'learning unreadiness' is the elimination of its birthplace, i.e., poverty. However, there is both a difference and choice between 'learning unreadiness' and 'learning readiness.'

Learning Readiness

Learning readiness is a very necessary educational skill as well as a skill beyond the arena of education. Learning readiness is not a static entity as itemized in Poverty & Despair versus Education & Opportunity [R 3-2]. Specifically, Figure 3-1 provides the basic dynamic between the need for [1] early- years consistent family advocacy and support and [2] the continuing advocacy and support throughout the cycle of life.

Some observations of Figure 4.1, *From Learning to Life,* are in order:

- Should any of the readiness factors of this model fail to provide sufficient support for the next step, then the overall readiness factor is compromised/weakened.
- The failure of multiple readiness factors results in insufficient readiness with little recovery opportunity.
- Conversely, if the readiness factors, individually *and* collectively, provide sufficient measures of readiness, this will translate directly to educational success and, subsequently, to a more successful and meaningful life.

From Learning to Life

Non-Poverty Environment	Poverty Environment
Prior to schooling	
Pre- and postnatal care; less stressful home; proper nutrition and sleep; more medical, dental, vision care; interactions, particularly verbal, with generally more educated adults; often safer and more nurturing home life; reading skill developed by being read to and having books; behavior development conducive to learning readiness	Less or no pre- and postnatal care; more stressful environment; may lack proper nutrition and sleep; less medical, dental, vision care; interactions, particularly verbal, with generally less educated adults; generally less safe and nurturing home life; less reading skill development by being read to and having books; likely less behavior development and school readiness
Pre-K, Elementary, Middle, and High School	
Continued resources supportive of learning, including more educated and likely nurturing parents; reading materials; technology; lessons in art, dance, and music; athletic activities; vacation experiences including museums, zoos, and aquariums; safer and less stressful home life	Few learning resources; often less educated, more stressed parents leading to harsh parenting and less nurturing; few outside learning experiences; stresses created by housing and food uncertainty; violence in the home and streets; untreated medical conditions; stresses lead to cortisol toxicity and impaired behavior/impulse control, concentration, and short-term memory
Life Outcomes	
High school diploma; college potential; stable employment income; healthier life	Under or unemployment; poverty level wages; few improvement opportunities; unstable housing and food; negative health issues; increased incarceration potential

Learning Readiness versus The Lack of Sufficient Learning Readiness

Figure 4.1 provides the more comprehensive and dramatic outcomes of the clearly contrasting realities of the education *and outcomes* readily available to those children 'beyond' poverty and those children of poverty . The former, for the most part, are prepared and move on to more promising endeavors and outcomes, whereas the latter suffer the bitter life-long consequences of poverty, e.g., lack of positive life and social skills, health issues, incarceration, unhealthy relationships, etc. This has been a continuing condition *for decade after decade after decade. Those students who live 'beyond' the limiting walls of poverty are prepared and move on to meaningful educations and more promising endeavors, states of health, and satisfaction in their journeys of life.*

There is little hope that poverty can be eliminated in the short term. However, over a longer term, if we can intentionally and appropriately support our students living in poverty so that they have the resources to move up the socioeconomic ladder, poverty will be significantly abated with the passage of time. Such an outcome is addressed in Chapter 10, *The Costs of Poverty*. The cost of maintaining families in poverty in America is astronomical. Aside from funding nutrition, housing, and medical support, America has one of the largest populations of the incarcerated in the world. If, as suggested here, America invested in the children in poverty, over time, America's standard of living would be enhanced for everyone.

> Children are apt to live up to what you believe of them.
>
> —LADY BIRD JOHNSON

CHAPTER 5

Poverty in the Classroom

> I choose to identify with the underprivileged, I choose to identify with the poor, I choose to give my life for the hungry, I choose to give my life for those who have been left out of the sunlight of opportunity.
>
> —DR. MARTIN LUTHER KING, JR.

Authors' note: Chapter 5 is really an expansion of Chapters 3 and 4 through the greater detail of enhancing the principle of 'connecting the dots.'

THIS CHAPTER ADDRESSES the educational environments built for non-poverty students in which a meaningful education is difficult, if not impossible, to acquire for students living in poverty. A meaningful education is one that is gained through a supportive academic environment and caregiving environment. This combination prepares the students to enter and advance through a Pre-K to 12 sequence. This informal and formal educational synergism also prepares the student for continued success in school and life. For most non-poverty students, the informal education received at home is a critical component in why these students arrive at school more "ready to learn." It is important to acknowledge that meaningful education is not as readily available to the children of poverty as it is for those children who do not live in poverty since that crucial informal component of developing learning readiness is often unavailable because of lack of affordability.

As noted, a "meaningful education" is not limited to formal schooling. Schools function in loco parentis, in place of the parents. Parents/caregivers provide advocacy and encouragement for education and play a vital role in the education of all children. If one looks at standardized test scores, the scores used to rate schools and teachers, there is a significant gap between more and less affluent children. There are volumes of research indicating this gap is not created in schools. The children of more socio-economically advantaged households enjoy myriad resources, activities, and models of educational success that complement and supplement their in-school learning. A literacy "learning gap" is apparent when a child enters Pre-K or kindergarten—long before there is any in-school contact. The more advantaged children, therefore, enter school more "learning ready" than their less advantaged peers. The advantages gained in the non-poverty homes do not end when a child enters school. Access to reading materials, technology, interactions with successful individuals, visits to museums and zoos, computer camps, and swim and dance lessons are just a few of the resources available to non-poverty children that continue to be provided to those children throughout their years in school. And are just as lacking in the homes of children living in poverty throughout their schooling.

In terms of "learning readiness," Ruby Payne [R 5-1], in her works on educating children living in poverty, notes the difference in how behavior is managed in homes at various socio-economic levels. Children in homes of lesser-educated parents tend to be more exposed to what Dr. Payne refers to as "harsh" parenting. They hear far more 'don'ts' and 'cant's'—far more negatives than positives. They are far less accustomed to types of more positive behavioral moderation techniques most likely to be used by a teacher who grew up in a non-poverty home—frustrating both themselves and their teachers.

To truly understand the history leading to the continuing state of sustained poverty in America [R 5-2], it is necessary to understand and acknowledge its genesis and history and, most importantly, its historical and continuing impact upon America and, especially, its children. Following the many years of slave trading in America, its imbedded racism and the absence of humanitarianism fueled the subsequent continuing growth of poverty , especially within the African-American communities across America. Lincoln's Executive Order of January 1, 1863, of the *Emancipation Proclamation* did provide the promise of 'freedom to all Americans'; however, the realities of freedom were not to come, albeit slowly and still incompletely, until decades later for African Americans. In 2010, James T. Patterson's *Freedom Is Not Enough* [R 5-3] reminds us that this action provided the initial cornerstone in America to 'freeing the slaves'; however, as the title and contents of Patterson's book state that 'cornerstone freedom is not enough." There must be more to do!

Ironically, slavery also led to abject poverty for many whites across the South. Slaves provided the labor that would have been provided by less educated whites in an agrarian economy. Tens of thousands of whites were forced into subsistence, living in makeshift shelters with no education and no medical care. There are vestiges of this poverty still evident in areas across the South. However, with the passage of time through the nineteenth and twentieth centuries and continuing in this century, it is the African-American population that became the predominant and most grievously treated population in America.

Earlier, in the summer of 1965, Senator-to-be Daniel Patrick Moynihan authored the *Moynihan Report* [R 5-4] *The Negro Family: The Case for National Action].* His premise was, "something must be done." He referred to the need for a strategy, a comprehensive plan.

President Johnson stated in his commencement address at Howard University , "Thus, it is not enough to open the gates of opportunity. All our citizens must have the ability to walk through those gates." Reflecting on those years, the civil rights movement was especially damaged by the resistance—sometimes violent—to the meaningful integration of the public school systems throughout America. Today's version of that 1965 statement could very well be, "All our citizens—not just some—

must have the opportunity to walk through those educational gates of opportunity so readily available to most Americans but often beyond reach for the children of poverty."

President Johnson, following Senator Moynihan's exhortations, created the War on Poverty. The program was comprehensive in that it covered education, housing, health, employment, and more. In ten years, the War on Poverty reduced poverty in the U.S. from 20% to 12%. It was the last time the gaps between more and less affluent students actually decreased. In 2020, as the successful components of the War on Poverty have been dropped to the wayside, the poverty rate for children in the U.S. is 21%.

You may ask, "What does this perspective of history have to do with education?"

As history has also abundantly demonstrated, the gates of opportunity for the children of poverty are at the entrances of those schools providing a meaningful education. History has demonstrated the futility of blaming schools for the learning gaps between lower and upper SES children. Twenty years of No Child Left Behind (NCLB) and its successor programs have had no impact on learning gaps. Most of the programs mistakenly targeted schools as the source of the gaps—rather than poverty. Schools not closing the gaps were labeled as "failing." Billions of dollars were spent on programs to "improve" schools and teachers. And the programs failed. National Assessment of Educational Progress [NAEP] data over twenty years clearly validates this point.

From Johns Hopkins University's Department of Sociology, Karl Alexander researched educational outcomes [R 5-5] in Baltimore for twenty-five years. Baltimore has a significant number of high-poverty neighborhoods. Alexander suggested the children of poverty keep pace with their non-poverty peers during the school day. However, standardized tests indicate they fall behind their non-poverty classmates over time. It's called *a learning gap*. Learning gaps are the difference between subsets of students on standardized test scores. Data have demonstrated that learning gaps tend to remain the same over the course of time, indicating some children in poverty are not losing ground, but neither are they closing the learning gap. Research suggests that most children in poverty fall behind during the summer when there is no school and when non-poverty children are offered more educationally positive home and community circumstances. There is less research on this advantage disparity throughout the school year. Soon, we will know the full implications of learning advantages enjoyed by non-poverty children during the period of COVID-19-caused virtual learning when children, regardless of economic class, spent much of their time at home. However, the non-poverty children, for the most part, had the advantage of resources supporting them at home learning.

If learning gaps are to be reduced, the focus needs to be on the students. The disparity, primarily, is in [1] learning deficits in the classroom and [2] the out-of-school environments and experiences when non-poverty students have far more resources to enhance their educations than the children of poverty. Thus, a learning gap is created by forces both within the classroom and outside of the schools. Not closing the learning gaps has been the primary determinant of a "failing school." Virtually all "failing schools" are in high-poverty areas. A more recent article [R 5-6] by Bailey Gerber offers a clear agreement with Alexander's comprehensive litany of related efforts.

The in-class learning deficits also have their roots in poverty. As noted elsewhere , poverty-related stresses produce cortisol. Overdoses of cortisol are toxic to the developing brain, resulting in less behavior control, impaired short-term memory and concentration—three critical components for learning.

The following questions and answers may shed some additional light and understanding of the spectrum of issues and challenges facing the children of poverty.

What exactly is poverty?

Poverty is historically treated and invoked as an economic metric often defined by *a household's income level [$$]; this metric only looks* *at the various strata of* poverty as a function of the annual income and population of the individual household. The abundance of available literature provides some insight into the different levels/dimensions of poverty, e.g., relative , deep , extreme , and absolute poverty. The American Psychological Association [Education & Socioeconomic Status Factsheet, July 2017 [R 5-7] provides the following comprehensive Socioeconomic Status [SES} definition: "SES encompasses not just income but also *educational attainment,* financial security, and subjective perceptions of social status and social class. Socioeconomic status can encompass quality of life as the opportunities and privileges afforded to people within society. Poverty, specifically, is not a single factor but rather is characterized by multiple physical and psychological stressors. Further, SES is a consistent and reliable predictor of a vast array of outcomes across the life span, including physical and psychological health. Thus, SES is relevant to all realms of behavioral and social science, including research, practice, *education,* and science."

However, there are even more facets/dimensions of 'poverty.' Specifically, '*The Rich and the Rest of US*' [R 5-8] is a 'poverty manifesto' complete with supporting statistical data as well as some very relevant and inspirational perspectives. This book addresses some additional dimensions of poverty with a strong linkage to the educational process for the children of poverty. These are the poverties of *opportunity, affirmation, courage, compassion,* and imagination. The author provides a quote by Marian Wright Edelman, President of the Children's Defense Fund:

> "If we think we have ours and don't owe any time or money or effort to help those left behind, then we are a part of the problem rather than the solution to the fraying social fabric that threatens all Americans."

What does the understanding of poverty have to do with public school education?

The current and historical status and quality of public school education really shape two very different populations characterized by those children who live in poverty and those children who live outside of the walls of poverty! While the latter, historically, are the fortunate recipients of a *meaningful education,* the children in poverty are not as fortunate.

The above-cited situation raises doubts about the belief and practice that 'one size of public education fits all.' One example cited earlier—one of many—is *Poverty & Despair versus Education & Opportunity* [Colella & Crowley, 2016, p. 75] [R 5-9]. 'Also, the practice of 'one size does fit all' pursued by educational administrators and educational 'engineers' may just be a contributing factor—even a significant factor—for leaving behind countless children and their opportunity to move forward.' A companion resource—rich in its own references—can be found at https://poverty-inequalities.com.

How do the effects of poverty impact the opportunity for a meaningful education?

Poverty is the primary deterrent to a child being able to take full advantage of the resources a school provides. The Adverse Childhood Experiences (ACE) scale (Kaiser Permanente, 1997) lists the injuries to a child's brain caused by childhood stresses and traumas. Additionally, children living in poverty suffer stresses from food, safety, and housing uncertainty; living with parents/caregivers stressed with finances and work; untreated medical, vision, and dental issues, among other stressors.

For the most part, the damage that accrues as a child moves up the ACE scale is something, more often than not, not the experiences of non-poverty children. While the damage extends to lifetime health, life expectancy, and other issues, the damage is most critical and problematic as a child moves through school.

The secretion of cortisol, the brain's 'fight or flight' chemical, is critical to survival. However, large doses of the stress spectrum over extended periods lead to biochemical, cellular, and physical changes in a child's brain. The result is behavior disorders, emotional instability, and issues with short-term memory and concentration—all critical factors in learning and learning readiness.

The child misbehaving may not have the ability to control his or her behavior. That part of the child's brain has been "bruised". The child may not retain what was learned yesterday. The child may have difficulty focusing. All are symptomatic of brain damage caused by stress.

These are the children deemed "not learning ready." *It is equally important to note that* teacher preparation programs, by and large, do not provide the training needed to relate to and teach these children, thereby exposing the children who are not " teacher-ready." Chapters 3 and 4, respectively, have already addressed the impact of students 'not being ready' to learn and the teachers 'not ready to teach' is an outcome that demands significant levels of classroom management, which, in turn, seriously minimizes the class time available for 'learning' and 'teaching'!

By now, one needs to wonder, "Can we do anything to help these children?" Can these children escape the downward spiral so often experienced by children whose brains have been altered by Adverse Childhood Experiences?

The answer is a resounding "Yes!" There is an antidote that actually reverses some of the brain damage caused by stress to the point that some of the damage can be reversed. And it is found in abundance in the most successful classrooms.

Nurturing and focused student mentoring is a cortisol antidote. In non-stressed homes, nurturing and mentoring are in the natural order of things. Not so in many poverty-troubled homes where the parents are as or more stressed than their children.

Unfortunately, the classroom behaviors of students who are not "learning ready" often deprive them of the benefits of a nurturing teacher. The disruptive, uncooperative student is not likely to be the "teacher's pet." The initial response of teachers not trained to educate children with poverty stress issues is, "I can't have that child in my classroom." Why do poor children—black, brown, or white—serve more suspensions than other students? They may the most difficult students to nurture while being most in need of nurturing.

As you will find throughout the book, the stress factors negatively impacting learning are one part of the genesis of learning gaps. The other major part is the aforementioned advantages of living in a home with parents who can complement and supplement school learning. The key solution to that issue is extended school time—longer days and/or longer school years for children living in poverty.

It is only possible to address these concerns and the casualties and corollary damages to all concerned if—and only if—there is an understanding of the debilitating impacts of poverty upon those students in the classroom as well as upon the effectiveness of teachers, principals, and administrators. These classrooms are truly the 'trenches of the education process.' This observation infers the outstanding need for a master plan [perhaps it could be entitled *As Long As It Takes*].

In that spirit and context, it is my goal to provide this book as awareness and guidance for those of you teachers-to-be and current teachers, as well as those administrators, shapers of educational policies, et al. responsible for transitioning these children out of poverty into a meaningful education!

First, it is necessary to acknowledge—and understand—the one-to-one geographical correlation between 'poor-performing schools' and areas of abject poverty.

Secondly, to move forward—whether an individual, a community, a corporation, or "Yes!, a nation!"—the first step is acknowledging the source/genesis of the problem/issue at hand. The United States Representative from Florida's 10th District, Val Demings, provided an exemplary but incisive perspective. With reference to the most recent protests, rioting, and looting throughout America in the Spring of 2020, she stated that progress with respect to countering/reducing/eliminating the pervasive institutionalized racism against African-Americans must first acknowledge 'those sins of the past' that are such an innate part of such racism [R 5-10] [Meet the Press, NBC, May 31, 2020]. It is an acceptable and effective staple and strategy that the initial step in 'escaping' from any debilitating situation is to understand and acknowledge the role of the enabling factors in the debilitating condition. This applies to an individual, a group,..., a nation, or any entity!

History reflections—there are many—also reflect earlier efforts providing unheard pleas and messages from the African-American community to address "those sins of the past" mentioned by Representative Demings. For example, Dubois, in September 1903—over a hundred years ago—wrote the *Talented Tenth* published in *The Negro Problem.* This article is an enlightening document from the post-Civil War days and is one of the earliest calls that *'something must be done'*—exactly the same message provided by Moynihan *fifty-seven years later in 1965.* One might even recall that Hubert H. Humphrey aptly provided the response to the 'civil-naysayers' of the 1960s: "There are those who say to you-we are rushing this issue of civil rights. I say we 172 years late." The spirit of this message is equally applicable to those who are reluctant—for whatever reason—to move forward in the direction of a solution that reduces/minimizes the impacts of the inequalities of poverty. Simply stated, *' Remove poverty, and you remove its inequalities.'* **Addressing the inequity in education so that all children and not just some have real opportunities for success regardless of their community's economics would be an excellent first step toward improving education!**

Authors Crowley & Colella, *Poverty & Despair versus Education & Opportunity* [R 5-9], also addressed the cartel of *poverty, racism, and violence* experienced earlier in Ferguson, Cleveland, Baltimore, and, currently, in Minneapolis and many other cities throughout America. The book also addresses the expectation that similar events are inevitable until the 'voices of the black community are heard *and addressed and acted upon!'*

However, this book introduces an educational 'model' that, by necessity and 'connecting the dots,' portrays the dynamic *connectivity* between poverty, learning readiness, teaching readiness, classroom behavior, and the necessity of classroom management. Additional insight is offered into the increasing and unsustainable costs in time, lost opportunities for millions of children each year, budgetary resources, and, most importantly, the life-long and unacceptable humanitarian costs.

There was a very poignant *Commentary* [R 5-11] in the November 27, 2015, *Providence Journal* by Joseph H. Crowley, with fifty years of relevant educational experience as a teacher, consultant, Executive Director of the Rhode Island Association of School Principals and a recognized expert in the arena of education. Mr. Crowley has long been one of the few 'voices' to address the devastating impact of *poverty* upon the opportunity for the children of poverty to attain a meaningful education. Conversely, there has been a growing chorus of 'voices' offering critiques, rationales, and misguided attention to America's 'failing schools' as the cause of educational deficits—however measured—of America's public school systems.

You can pose the question: "Is this collective blame for the 'failing schools' really a fair assessment in the light of all those teachers, principals, administrators, et al. who have consistently provided outstanding performances throughout the years?"

That said, a very relevant example of these two 'schools of thought' can be found within the following paraphrasing of the several summary observations from his cited [R 5-11] and two follow-up editorials: *'No excuses'* [R 5-12] [December 2, 2015] and, almost four years later, *'Models for school reform'* [R 5-13] [August 2, 2019].

Commentary [R 5-11] of November 27, 2015:

- PARCC [Partnership for the Assessment of Readiness for College and Careers] was reported as "Stunning." However, six of the top eight PARCC scores belong to the four districts with the wealthiest, i.e. non-poverty, students. Interestingly, eight of the lowest scores came from the four districts with the neediest students.
- There existed a consensus amongst many, e.g., federal government and state and local officials, that low scores in high-poverty districts are the outcome of "failing" schools.
- Studies, e.g., Wallace foundation, infer that outside-of-school-activities shape 40% of students' learning variables.
- Could it be that the schools in neighborhoods of *poverty* are identified as "failing" schools because their teachers were expected to compensate for the embedded poverty-driven socio-economic disadvantages and disabilities?
- Could it be that the 'gaps in educational achievement between high and low-SES children are symptomatic of conditions created by poverty?
- **Could a meaningful education be the best road out of a life in poverty, while living in poverty is the biggest roadblock to a meaningful education?**

Editorial [R 5-12] of December 2, 2015, 'No Excuses':

- This Editorial of 12/2/15 does state that *poverty* is a challenge, but it must not be made an excuse. However, in concert with Crowley's Commentary of 11/27/15, it does state that the poor and minority students deserve an opportunity to partake of the American dream and, most importantly, that the barriers that deny the children of poverty that opportunity so readily available to those who live beyond the virtual walls of poverty need to be *dismantled*.

- The relevance of the editorial title *No Excuses* to the email contents does have merit, but it is vague, at best with respect to the linkage between poverty and the educational status of the children living in poverty.

Editorial [R 5-13] of August 2, 2019, 'Models for school reform':

- '*Models for school reform*' provides general guidance for the remaking of Rhode Island's public schools. However, this editorial's closing statement is the "giving poor and minority students a real shot at the American Dream is the civil rights challenge of our time.
- There exists an implication that principals and schools could take care of the learning gaps created by poverty. An appropriate response follows: 'Why, in the fifteen years since NCLB, have schools and principals failed to close the 'learning gaps' at all? If poverty is the real reason behind learning gaps, how will principals and schools resolve the problem with the resources available to them?
- It certainly seems that both editorials are in agreement with Crowley's *Commentary*!
- The belief that 'failing schools' are the real problem; however, this belief dismisses what the data/information on higher-income versus lower-income districts infer.
- **Educational spoke-persons have operated under the misguided notion that the learning gaps are symptomatic of 'failing schools.' When one assumes these schools are the problem, one looks to schools for the solution. One cannot treat symptoms and expect the real problem to go away.**

Why the emphasis on poverty? Haven't the implemented programs already addressed and successfully reduced the learning gaps?

We have seen that a series of national education strategies and programs were implemented with the best of intentions. However, they consumed significant time or budget without having a meaningful and lasting impact on the education of children. For example, these programs promised to reduce the significant learning gaps between those living in poverty and those who do not: an example of the clear difference between these two student populations. More than likely, the effects of some of these programs enabled diversions and compromises to, historically, the successful educational practices and protocols.

NO CHILD LEFT BEHIND [NCLB] and *RACE TO THE TOP [RTTT]* mistakenly assumed 'learning gaps' arose from the schools. They do not. 'Learning gaps' between higher and lower SES [Socio-economic status] directly reflect what those children living beyond the virtual walls of poverty learn from their environments—and what poorer children do not. NCLB and RTTT have done monumental damage to our public education systems: demoralized educators and teachers from their chosen profession, dissuaded candidate teachers from becoming teachers, created false impressions that charter schools are better and ruined the confidence and trust of the public and policy makers in our schools.

More specifically, children living in poverty do not do as well on standardized tests as their non-poverty peers because these latter students come from home and community environments, providing educational advocacy and advantages reflected in test outcomes. Again, the reality of two very different student populations, i.e., for children in poverty to test as well as their non-poverty peers, they would need to have similar advantages as those peers. This dichotomy difference is quite analogous to the realization in the latter part of the twentieth century that the SAT tests also gave an advantage to the non-poverty peers and, conversely, a disadvantage to the children of poverty. Prior to this belated realization, there existed a marked unfairness and disadvantage to the children of poverty. Opportunity lost! Public schools have been under assault since President George W. Bush kidnapped President Johnson's Elementary and Secondary Education Act [ESEA] and renamed it No Child left behind [NCLB]. Johnson had created ESEA as part of his War on Poverty, which decreased the 'learning gaps' between socioeconomic [SES] because it correctly identified *poverty* as being the problem. President Obama joined the 'War on Public Schools' in his Race to the Top [RTTT] initiative.

This effort provided $4.3 billion for states that would fix "failing schools." These billions were added to the billions provided via ESEA. The Washington Post, in a recent article, posted this headline: "Obama administration spent these billions to fix 'failing schools,' and it didn't work!"

At this point, according to the National Assessment of Educational Progress [NAEP], known as the nation's report card, provided the following: from 2003 to 2015, NAEP test scores improved for all students by a modest amount. However, what can be said about the children living in poverty who make up the population of "failing schools"? 8th-grade math gaps are unchanged; 8th-grade literacy, 4th-grade math, and 4th-grade literacy gaps all decreased by one point on a 500-point scale in those twelve years.

Johns Hopkins University found that the learning gap grew most during the summer vacation, not during the school year. *It is living in poverty, which creates the symptoms that make it appear that it is the schools that are failing. "Failing schools are symptomatic of large enrollments of children living in poverty. It is also symptomatic of the culture of poverty that is giving rise to the increasing need for classroom management!"* The underlying issue that needs to be addressed is poverty.

The only industrialized nations with more children in poverty than the US are Turkey, Greece, Israel, and Mexico. America can increase its test scores by reducing the number of children living in poverty—which exceeds 20%. Schools need added resources for extended day and school year programs as well as summer programs to counter the increase in learning gaps for the children of poverty.

Daniel Akst, Newsday, [R 5-14] columnist and commentary contributor, *"Poverty, not bad teachers, most plagues our schools,"* is a convert. Diane Ravitch, former United States Undersecretary of Education and an education consultant, is a convert. Canada and Australia, two countries with similar immigration demographics to ours, have long held the belief that poverty issues must be addressed to improve educational outcomes.

Canada and Australia, whose students outperform their American counterparts (see the 2010 Program for International Student Assessment—PISA—results), have adopted the attitude the schools cannot do it alone. Even in this country, successful programs such as the Harlem Children's Zone extend support well beyond the schoolhouse door. There is virtually no research supporting approaches to improving learning for children in poverty, which has focused entirely on teachers and administrators.

What does work, as has been found in a number of studies, is early childhood interventions and extended school day and year offerings. Interactions with families that bring the families into the schools and the support into the home. Medical and dental support is offered. Schools as havens are arguably where there is at least a single adult a child can relate with. (Should anyone think interventions do not work, consider the education consequences of eliminating lunch and breakfast programs.)

Whereas there may be schools performing at less than desirable levels, schools and teachers in areas serving high populations of students in poverty are not, as Akst argues, the basic problem. They are not, for the most part, "underperforming" schools. They are, on the other hand, schools serving high concentrations of children underperforming due to poverty-related issues. Schools, or even the entire society, are not likely to address the underlying issue of poverty. What schools and we, as a society, can do is identify poverty as the real problem and address the impediments to learning associated with poverty.

We can stop demonizing and demoralizing good teachers and administrators by blaming them for conditions they did not create, nor have we given them the tools to overcome. Changing staff and shifting students to other schools merely masks the real problem. It's a 'feel good' illusion based on "somebody's doing something." It creates a negative perception of educators and our public schools that is totally underserved.

Non-poverty children are being provided resources that enhance their learning processes and which are reflected in standardized test scores—reading materials, using technology, visits to zoos, field trips, museums, aquariums, science fairs, travel, and even the advantages of having more family and community environments. To level the playing field, children in poverty need more school/class time-extended days and school years. Their school day can be structured to provide more contact with educationally and developmentally trained adults while being exposed to activities they may not likely experience in their respective home environments—for example, art and music, swimming and sports, and visits to educational sites.

Author Colella has provided [1] a historical background of slavery and its inherent racism and [2] the impact of the recent fifteen-year ministry [1995-2011] serving the families, and especially, their children in *Let's Start With the Children* [R 5-15]. This book provides a realistic, expanded example and insight into the dichotomy between the children of poverty and those who are not. It is important to note that these two student populations strongly require very different educational requirements but share some common ground. The parents, more so those in generational poverty, may not be able to value education and impart this, both subliminally and otherwise, to their children. This has a two-pronged impact. The children may not see education as valuable, and the parents may be less likely to work with the school to improve their children's educational outcomes and, by extension, the opportunity to learn some necessary life skills.

Author Kimberly Deninger offers the following: "It is somewhat ironic that my classroom experience of the last six years has been for both the students and the teachers—very difficult, even chaotic, educationally, emotionally and physically challenging. Despite those few 'magical moments' of connection with far too few of my students, I cannot accept the collateral personal and educational damage to so many students; I find this classroom environment *unfair, underserved, unnecessary, and unacceptable* [R 5-15]. However, via some reverse reflection, I acknowledge and understand that these children in my classrooms are products of their respective environments of poverty that are equally *unfair, undeserved, unnecessary, and unacceptable."*

I would be irresponsible if I did not mention that the 'saving grace' for each and all of my students—whom I love dearly—is my inner sense that each and all really 'want to learn.' However, supportive classroom conditions simply may not always exist to sustain their 'urge to learn.'

The conflicts between and among student needs, student behaviors, and the available classroom resources to resolve these conflicts have led to too many teachers leaving the classroom and seeking alternate professions. More on this in Chapter 8.

Making Good Humans, Getting Parents On Board

—TARYN B. CLEGG [R 5-15]

CHAPTER 6

Classroom Environments

Following my graduation with my BA degree in Elementary and Special Education, I had anticipated a reasonably smooth transition into the teaching profession. My early years as a teacher were very challenging—very challenging—to me professionally, emotionally, and physically! I wasn't really prepared for the educational road ahead. Fortunately, I had the guidance, support, advocacy, and mentoring of a successful career educator during those very difficult early years as a 'teacher.' I am now in my ninth year of teaching and still preparing myself for each and every day in the classroom.

At the beginning of my second year of teaching, my mentor suggested that I create a daily journal summarizing the events of the day—the good, the bad, and the ugly, but also those special positive but rare moments for a student and myself! My journal took an entire school year to complete and is entitled 'Hope Anchors the Soul,' and it really represents the genesis for writing this entire book and its subsequent growth.

I have selected those journal entries that best reflect the students and my classroom environment for the entire academic year. It is important to note that Chapters 1 through 5 are the necessary context for Chapter 6! And chapters 7, 8, 9, 10 provide the continuity and completeness of the overall message of this book!

—AUTHOR KIMBERLY DENINGER

Daily Quotations from *Hope Anchors the Soul*

(Second year of teaching)

August 31, 2015: Brilliant moment for N., rough and tumble kid, he bonded with L. They both worked hard (and silently) together! Z. told Ms. B., "My daddy says you have to heat up my fries [McDonalds] for me!" Ha! No!

September 14, 2015: Huge step—tried centers for the first time. Maybe a 7 out of 10 ☺ So we will keep practicing.

September 16, 2015: Decent day ☺ Started journals with the spelling words. And finally got through ELA and math centers. Just so tired from yesterday.

October 1, 2015: They were awesome in the hall today—4 compliments in 10 minutes! Fun Friday and treats for them.

October 13, 2015: So Mom swears that he took his medicine!

October 14, 2015: Great morning—crap afternoon…

October 22, 2015: C.'s grandfather was very apologetic about his grandson's behavior.

November 6, 2015: Introducing them to a new sub should be interesting. She has worked in the mental health field—she should fit right in. lol!

November 12, 2015: Had a super awesome lesson where the babies used and explored base 10 blocks. It's nice to see them working well together every once in a while.

November 13, 2015: J. is suspended for fighting—and C. has been asleep for the last hour.

November 16, 2015: They are only going to get crazier. Sweet mercy!

November 17, 2015: I am getting another new kid, which puts my official total @ 23, plus A., who is in here because the sub can't handle him, so I'm @ 24! And at the busiest time of the year! I don't know if I want to scream or cry.

December 1, 2015: The principal does not know what I'm saying to him! Test scores are going to be so low :o(. 6 ESOL + 3 unlabeled)
December 8, 2015: Dare I say it—a good day.
December 10, 2015: I'm tired of them yelling!
December 14, 2015: Y. is going to end up being suspended.
December 15, 2015: Got all but 9 of my RRR tests done! Sweet.
December 17, 2015: They won't listen and are just so mean to each other.
December 18, 2015: Lollipops keep their mouths closed!
January 8, 2016: TGIF!
January 11, 2016: J. pulled out one of his 'gold' teeth, so that was interesting.
January 13, 2016: K. punched I. b/c I. broke his toy.
January 19, 2016: Started F. on her sticker chart—so hopefully that will work.
January 25, 2016: Had the kids write a note to me saying something that they wished that I knew…most of them were "I love you's" but some where actually facts about themselves. Definitely something to keep doing!
January 29, 2016: Spoke to H.'s Dad about him slapping his classmates. He got picked up b/c he had a breakdown during math.
February 1, 2016: S.'s mom told D. that she could not be more thrilled that I have been her teacher for 2 years.
February 4, 2016: They can't stop shouting!
February 10, 2016: Probably the worst bday ever. Ask for one date for them to pull it together—HA! Not even close.
February 12, 2016: They didn't really do any of their work—but they listened better.
February 19, 2016: Sent K. & A. to principal by 8:30—kicking and screaming @ friends during a spelling test—isn't ok…
February 25, 2016: Had to jump over a table to stop two of the boys from playing tag in the classroom.
February 26, 2016: One of those days you go home in tears.

March 1, 2016: Pretty good—rearranged the room and that seems to have helped.

March 17, 2016: I have had 3 students picked up for fighting…

March 29, 2016: Y. asked me: "If it wasn't illegal, would you tape everyone's mouths shut?" HA! YES!

March 31, 2016: H. attacked L. again—had to physically carry him out this time.

April 1, 2016: "Hey, your shoe is untied! April Fools! HAHAHA!"

April 4, 2016: Y. asked me why I let A. do whatever he wants—um no!—he doesn't listen.

April 11, 2016: I think we have finally hit our 4th Q stride.

April 13, 2016: Started my daily countdown…40 days to go!

April 14, 2016: The butterflies are hatching, 7 out of 10. ☺ Kinder came to see—very exciting. Rain has been bad so we'll let them out next week…

April 15, 2016: We taught the other first floor classes about our butterflies. They did pretty well for their first presentation.

April 26, 2016: Going to have to spend an afternoon setting up new centers…they need a change and I need a break.

April 28, 2016: So many meltdowns—what the hell.

May 4, 2016: I can't wait till I work in a school that actually appreciates its teaching staff…26 days to go!

May 6, 2016: M.'s mom brought me a gift basket & balloon. ☺ He isn't even my kid but she knows how hard this job can be. She knows I love chocolate.

May 10, 2016: I stayed past time to present a jacket to the only student in my class who met the criteria.

May 13, 2016: But gave out progress reports…A. freaked out and hid under the table …19 days to go!

May 20, 2016: P.'s dad called me stupid b/c I wouldn't give him 'his son'; sorry! But I have no idea who you are.

May 25, 2016: Y. told me to wear my dress *and* some makeup to go on a date.

June 2, 2016: Got emails about the playground closing—kids broke the fence.

June 3, 2016: Centers and moves b/c that's where we're at!

June 6, 2016: Takes forever to do anything—so tired!

June 8, 2016: Field Day was a complete bust...nothing was set up; the game directions blew away, and not enough supervision! The games were meant for groups of 6-10...I had 18 students by myself.

June 9, 2016: A.'s Dad was shot & killed this morning! Heartbreaking!

In summary, these entries really reflect the realities of our classroom environment!

My journal reflects my perseverance, efforts, and successes...and my hope!

Author Kim also completed her second journal entitled: 'Nevertheless she persisted'; her entries follow:

(Sixth year of teaching; grades K-12 as special education)

I am at a different school! Year 6, my last year?

It is October 9, 2020, week 7 of school...

My classroom is deteriorating at a rapid pace...

I am responsible for 22 students across Kinder, 1st and 2nd grades...

One of my students is out on a 10-day suspension for assaulting a pregnant staff member. He should have been at a better location at the beginning of the year, but he did 'so well' at summer school [3 hours/ day] they sent him back...we were crushed.

Another of my high flyers is ED [emotionally disturbed] , MLD [multiple learning disabilities]; also has seizures and a recently found mass on his brain... (heart-breaking!)

We hope to get him into a therapeutic setting that can provide him the therapy and medications he needs...

So it's safe to say my working conditions are not ideal...I did not sign up to be an ED teacher...I signed up to teach reading & math skills...

Instead, I'm required to use restraint & seclusion on an hourly basis...

*The following in my log of reasons that my new principal thinks I'm unprofessional:

- I took a personal day without permission ahead of time.
- I gave my coworkers honest answers when they asked me how I'm doing...
- I moved a table out of my classroom without the permission of the Administrative Assistant.

(Fifth year of teaching; grade three)

October 11, 2019

They got on tables with wheels today..."No...stop...get down... unsafe." My surprise expression when they moved. PRICELESS :o)

I'm tired of being hit, kicked, sworn at, etc.

One of my students was in crisis...I called for support...no one came...I called again.

I cried twice today...I'm so frustrated.

I love my boys but I don't know how much more I can take.

October 16, 2019

I could not get it together.

I had a few friends check in on me, and I had another panic attack.

Explain to me how, in the span of 43 minutes, I went from cuddling my kinders to putting one into a restraint so he wouldn't possibly dash out into the bus loop...

October 29, 2019

In yet another attempt to call a student's mother...the phone in his bookbag rang! So, yes, the mother of a 9 -year-old boy with epilepsy & mood disorders put the boy's own number as the emergency contact... WOW!

November 8, 2019

Day from hell....

I'm tired of having a headache...

I'm not sure this is worth it.

November 22, 2019:

There have been some improvements.

It has been 3 weeks since the principal suspended the 3 destructive/dangerous personalities. HOWEVER...

Today, my principal decided that "now that the dust has settled," they can go back together.

My lead asked if I was consulted—again HA!

December 12, 2019:

It has been one hell of a week!

Monday: we had HR come to the school to investigate the 3rd-grade class—why?—Because one of the teachers, who believes she is a Wiccan, has cast a poisoning spell on her teammates since she dislikes them so much.

Tuesday: covered the Kinder most of the day. Temporarily forgot what it was like to have 6 -year-old kids calling each other crackheads... (It was a good day.)

Wednesday: a 3rd grader TORE UP a classroom—like every piece of paper, every pencil, EVERYTHING! And to think I asked for the 3rd grade...

January 31, 2020:

Any teacher will tell you that this is the longest month of the year. Yikes!

February 20, 2020:

R. is losing his mind...so it climaxed this morning when he bit 4 separate adults in 40 minutes...insisted that my friend & I go get her arm checked…turns out he broke the skin, and now she is on antibiotics. Meanwhile, his mom is pissed since this is his first time being suspended when he has bitten staff on multiple occasions before…there is just no winning.

Dr. Colella [one of the three authors] provided this to Kim:

"Kim: just a question for you: from my reading and understanding the challenge of your excessively challenging classroom environments, I'm wondering if, for your school experiences, was there always an unbelievable lack of staff and educational management skills, competence, support, etc. It appears that your situation and experience are wholly and totally unacceptable!! We can have a conversation about this and your thoughts, OK? And we did!"

February 29, 2020:

Mom did not show up to his BIP review [with a team of 8! b/c it slipped her mind to call, and let me know she couldn't make it]

Girl, I called you 2 weeks ago, and you said, "no problem."

A colleague is continuing to tattle to the administration about the issues between 6 of her boys and one 'autistic' student.

We have all applied for new jobs. As much as the girls and I want to stay together, we can't work in a disrespectful environment.

March, 2020:

I miss teaching.

I miss building lessons & following them through.

I miss creating co-teaching, having a friend to bounce off of.

I miss accessing all my resources.

I miss incorporating technology into my classroom.

I miss not having anxiety sweats.

I miss not needing medication to keep calm.

I miss reading stories to my kids.

I miss using manipulatives in my lessons.

I miss having my pencil cup on my desk.

I miss wearing decent shoes and clothes.

I miss being able to focus on the needs of more than one child.

I miss being able to take a day off-guilt free.

I miss having classroom decorations.

I miss having door decorations.

I miss having the energy to workout.

I miss the energy to socialize outside of school.

I miss the kindness of parents.

I miss being able to talk to colleagues without fear of parents or administrators POPPING up!

March 18, 2020:

Day 6 of quarantine. I'm trying to decide how worried I should be about my students…

Part of me says 'no' since parents are always telling me how to do my job—now I really shouldn't tell them how to do theirs.

Part of me says 'yes' since, more than likely, some at home won't be getting the attention they need.

Looks like we'll be closed for two weeks.

I'm looking forward to a fresh new school year.

Author's Note on 'Connecting the Dots'

What does *'connecting the dots'* really mean? Basically, it's not rocket science, i.e., the more connections that you can 'see/visualize,' the more you know about those 'parts,' i.e., the *functions* of a particular system, the more you can understand about the performance of that particular system! The failure to rely on a reliable and proven system model inevitably leads to tremendous costs of time, budget, and performance failures, as well as humanitarian and social costs.

The intent and goal of this approach are remarkedly appropriate for the educational system—any educational system—*but especially for the educational realities of the children of poverty who, by and large, are denied a meaningful education! A situation that has existed for decade after decade... after decade.*

Simply put, the more *relevant* 'dots' that you can envision, the 'greater your knowledge of the system'—for example, within the overall context of this book, in ineffective and failing educational systems for the children living in poverty!

To that point, Kim Deninger is currently expanding her academic education of her already completed BA and Master's Degrees to a second Master's Degree in 'Behavioral Science.' One could even call this current effort a 'dot.' The forthcoming Chapter 8, *Systemic & Inclusive Educational Model: Linkages & Dynamics,* developed by Authors Deninger, Crowley & Colella, portrays a 'starting point' to provide much-needed assistance to those long-neglected children of poverty!

CHAPTER 7

Classroom Management & Teacher Leadership

> These Kids Are Out of Control... [R 7-1]
>
> —H. MILNER ET AL.

Overview: The Process of 'Classroom Management'

THERE IS AN ABUNDANCE of available literature, information, and perspectives relevant to 'classroom management,' e.g., a wide variety of plans, styles, strategies, philosophies, techniques, and creative approaches—each shaped by classroom-specific classroom management requirements across the classrooms of the educational world. One outcome of the research can be had by Googling 'classroom management' and exploring the growing number of available links and books. Most sources are experientially based and informative, and most reflect a wide spectrum of successful educational initiatives within the classrooms of America. It is important to acknowledge success via their respective positive impacts on both the learning readiness of the students and, of equal importance, the teaching readiness of the teachers. However, it is equally and critically important to note that the greater requirement for time for classroom management translates directly to a decrease in the classroom time available for enhancing the learning readiness of the students and the teaching readiness for those teachers in such classrooms. Simply put, classroom management techniques need to be, time-wise, intrinsically woven into the educational process in order to minimize that valuable time lost for teaching and learning.

There is a *Wikipedia* [R 7-2] article that provides a comprehensive and meaningful definition of 'classroom management'; a partial excerpt follows:

> *"Classroom management"* is a term teachers use to describe the process of ensuring that classroom lessons run smoothly without *disruptive behavior from students compromising the delivery of instruction. The term also implies the prevention of disruptive behavior preemptively, as well as effectively responding to it after it happens.
>
> It is a difficult aspect of teaching for many teachers. Problems in this area cause some teachers to leave teaching. In 1981, the US National Educational Association reported that 36% of teachers said that they would not go into teaching if they had to decide again. A major reason was negative student attitudes and discipline [R 7-3]. With the passage of time, the additional reasons include a lack of advocacy and support from the school management staff.
>
> [*Author's note: the issue of disruptive [classroom] behavior is often a direct outcome of learning unreadiness and the lack of advocacy and support for education in poverty-driven family/community environments.]
>
> Classroom management is crucial in classrooms because it enables curriculum development, develops best teacher practices, and puts them into action. Classroom management can be explained as the actions and directions teachers use to create a successful learning environment [R 7-4]. To ensure all students receive the best education, it would seem beneficial for educator programs to spend more time and effort in ensuring educators and instructors are well-versed in classroom management.

Teachers may focus on learning classroom management because higher education programs do not put an emphasis on classroom management in a challenging classroom setting. The focus is on creating a conducive learning atmosphere for the student [R 7-5].

These tools enable teachers to have the resources available to properly and successfully educate upcoming generations and ensure future success as a nation [R 7-6]. Once a teacher loses control of their classroom, it becomes increasingly more difficult for them to regain that control. Also, research from Berliner [R 7-7], J.L Graden, J.E. Zins, M.J. Curtis [R 7-8] and J.E. Brophy, T.L. Good, M.C. Wittrock [R 7-9] show that the time a teacher must take to address and correct misbehavior caused by poor classroom management skills results in a lower rate of academic engagement in the classroom. From the student's perspective, effective classroom management involves clear communication of behavioral and academic expectations, consistent and fair application of those expectations as well as a cooperative learning environment [R 7-10].

The following commentaries from each of the three references are provided that directly resonate with this chapter. Individually and collectively, there is an added value to fully understand some of the added dimensions of classroom management:

[1] ***"These Kids Are Out of Control: Why We Must Reimagine Classroom Management for Equity"*** **[R 7-1]**

Amazon.com provides the authors' systemic message of their book: *"If you're looking for a book on how to 'control' your students, this isn't it." This is a book on what classroom teaming could be if we aspire to co-create more culturally responsive and equitable environments—environments that are safe, affirming, learner-centered, intellectually challenging, and engaging—if we create the kind of places where students want to be.*

Amazon.com also provides nine quite powerful and relevant book reviews. Each reflects the common ground for the diverse student population of interest, i.e., urban, those trapped in the cradle-to-prison pipeline, diverse backgrounds and personal histories, and justice-oriented classroom management. Three of these reviews follow:

- "These Kids are out of Control shines a light on the importance of classroom management in urban schools while appropriately placing it in the full context of urban education. The authors expertly provide a firm research base upon which they offer evidence-based and practical strategies that urban educators can incorporate. They go into detail on how, why, and what these strategies look like to better prepare and support urban teachers in classroom management. As a teacher educator, I know I will definitely incorporate these strategies listed in this book to help my pre-service teachers understand how to better manage urban classrooms. Researchers and teacher educators alike will find this book useful for pushing forward the field of classroom management in urban schools while equipping teachers and administrators with the day-to-day skills needed to succeed." Andrew Kwok, Ph.D., Assistant Professor, College of Education, published on February 7, 2018 [R 7-12].

- "If you are an educator who wants to resist and dismantle the cradle-to-prison pipeline, this is your manifesto. Deeply researched, accessibility written, and powerfully applied, this book demonstrates not just why we need to make justice the goal of our classroom management practices but it also shows how we get it done. Read this, and you'll know what to do to make our schools and classrooms more hopeful, critical, responsive, and equitable." Eric Toshalls, Research Director, Published on February 20, 2018 [R 7-13].

- "Today's educators must meet the daily challenge of providing quality teaching for students from wide, diverse backgrounds and personal histories. While research on managing classrooms has provided some guidance, significant gaps in our understanding remain, such as the lack of in-depth theoretical and foundational knowledge about issues of race, culture, and inequity as they impact schooling. The authors have given us vital insights into these important factors. I believe this book is one of the most significant contributions to research on classroom management. It is a MUST read and belongs in every educator's library." Carolyn M. Evertson, Ph.D., Professor of Education, Emerita, Published on February 2, 2018 [R 7-14].

[2] ***Small Victories, The Real World of a Teacher, Her Students, and their High School,* Samuel G. Freedman** [**R 7-15**]

This book is a remarkable book because it portrays the journey of the English Instructor, Jessica Siegel, in the challenging educational arena that, according to the book's author, Samuel G. Freedman, "seems like a disaster with walls-old, urban, overcrowded, and overwhelmingly minority on Manhattan's Lower East Side ." Also, "ranked among the worst 10 percent of high schools in the state—yet 92 per cent of its graduates go on to higher education." The foundation for this remarkable educational success is Siegel's dramatic *humanization* of the education crisis. Simply put, Siegel understands that there is *always opportunity* imbedded within a crisis, but only if one has the vision to see and acknowledge it and, then, act positively and creatively on it!

[3] ***Seven Key Elements for Effective Classroom Management*** [**R 7-16**]

Across time, students, and classroom environments, these seven basic but key elements are portrayed as 'common ground' for primary school teachers, their disciplinary methods, and behavioral expectations:

- Classroom Design
- Roles

- Discipline
- Scheduling
- Organization
- Instructional Technique
- Communication

It is shown in Chapter 7 [*Elements of Teaching and Teacher* [R 7-17] *Leadership*] that another *unique* and *intangible* factor comes into play in every classroom across the educational spectrum. As Jessica Siegel [*Small Victories* [R 7-18]] demonstrated, i.e., the *humanization* of the educational process. This *unique* and *intangible* factor comes from within and doesn't lie within course descriptions, class schedules, or other rote-oriented procedures. It always lies within the individual teacher who is consistently successful by any and all metrics.

Educational Preparation for Teachers-to-be: Undergraduate and Graduate Programs

As suggested previously, there exists an abundance of literature addressing some specific aspects of classroom management and its potential positive and negative impacts on the students' learning skills and the teachers' instructional skills.

There is also an abundance of singular courses throughout America's many colleges and universities offering such courses both on the undergraduate and graduate levels. There are also 'pieces' of classroom management topics that can be found within both undergraduate and graduate education courses and programs. Some basic research has indicated that—despite the proliferation of books, articles, papers, et al. addressing the topic of classroom management—there exist relatively few systemic concentrations of classroom management embedded within both undergraduate and graduate education courses and programs. One might even ask, "Why aren't there more minors or concentrations for the teachers-to-be who might just find their inaugural teaching profession assignment in those schools in which classroom management is, historically, a significant issue, e.g., schools in areas of sustained poverty?"

One may even ask why a significant percentage [36%] of teachers polled reflect that classroom management remains the dominant issue that motivates teachers to regret entering the teaching profession upon completing either their undergraduate or graduate educational programs.

A related question is, what motivates the individual teacher to opt out of the teaching profession? Still another question: Is there a nationwide teacher shortage, and is anything being done about it? Three references immediately come to mind: [1] as mentioned in Chapter 2, *Understanding Teacher Shortages* [R 7-19], [2] *Are Teacher Shortages Worse Than We Thought* [R 7-20] and *The Teacher Shortage Is Real, Large and growing Worse Than We Thought* [R 7-21].

However, the point is missed that *the individual teachers know their respective selves and the kids in* their respective classrooms!"

Some Added Insight Into Teacher Leadership for Learning & Teaching Readiness

Author's perspective: In Chapter 1, I mentioned that my undergraduate teaching education simply did not prepare me for the real challenges of the learning and teaching challenges of the classroom. Chapter 2, then, provides a more comprehensive insight into the lack of *teacher preparation* imbedded in some-perhaps, too many-undergraduate programs. A lesson learned: there is not a single strategy/protocol that will address this lack of teacher preparation. *Teaching preparation* requires, of course, a more comprehensive curriculum to better address the realities of learning unreadiness, e.g., *teaching readiness* [Chapter 4], effective *classroom management, and teacher leadership*!

How do your students 'feel' when they come into your classroom in the morning? How do you want them to feel? What needs to change for your students to feel that way?

As a novice teacher, it took me several years to learn that even if you can have all the fun decorations, job charts, and reinforcement systems set up for the first day of school, they will [to varying degrees] get blown apart on the first day of school [and those to follow]. In college, they taught us to write classroom rules and [logically] how to set expectations for kindness and physical safety. However, none of what I had during my first year of teaching went as planned, and I was just *not prepared* to adjust and recalculate my classroom needs on the spot as well as the students' needs. I previously mentioned, and as many of you know, how students had to be taught to sit on chairs with their feet on the floor and how some students needed explicit teaching on conversational turn-taking and sharing with others. I had to back way up in the developmental timeline to create and [try to] establish classroom expectations, routines, and incentives. I will repeat that it did not go well! I had to rely heavily on my coworkers for both emotional and [at times] physical assistance and support. Are you even a first-year teacher if you do not have a crying session in the middle of the school day?

Eventually, I was able to set in place a somewhat structured outline for the twenty-seven kindergarteners I had in my care. But we did keep our heads above water. Every year since has been a process to learn what the kiddos coming into my classroom need, what they are able to do, and how I can help them learn 'how to do' as originally anticipated.

I had and still have students who come from difficult, even unthinkable, family and community situations requiring more structure and consistency than what most would feel is necessary.

We know that our classrooms need to be a place where our students can feel safe and secure in themselves, feel valued as a part of the group, and feel acknowledged by the teacher.

Establishing a positive classroom environment is a lot of hard work, especially in these post-pandemic times. We need to reteach or possibly teach students—for the first time—how to interact with others, how to take turns, how to express themselves, and all while working to make the 18-25 of those personalities coexist in a 30 x 40 foot space, and all of that shifting every time a student moves or enrolls. Once we know the needs of our students, we must develop a classroom management system and an effective leadership strategy that helps the class work together like a team. What do these students need to work together and be successful in school, community, and beyond? How can I build that for them? Is there an answer to this question that needs to be addressed in the undergraduate teacher programs?

One basic technique for achieving comprehensive and effective classroom management enabling both positive learning and teaching readiness outcomes is to [1] draw from one's personal experience *as a student,* [2] model one's classroom strategies after those used by other teachers and oneself successfully; it's always a good strategy to 'copy success' and [3] do a self-assessment on a continuing basis by understanding the answers to two questions: the first is "What am I doing right?" and the second: "What am I *not* doing right?"

The following factors represent some experience-based techniques for the improvement of classroom management. The individual teacher is encouraged to modify this list of factors and shape it for their respective classroom management needs and abilities.

- Create your own list of [1] those classroom activities that you thought were positive for you as a student [probably not a long list] and [2] those classroom activities that did not make your life and progress as a student as enriching and comfortable as it should have been. Simply put, emphasize and practice the 'positive' attributes and avoid the 'negative' ones.

- Are you on time for class? Better yet, do you arrive at class early for informal interaction with your students? This is a unique opportunity to better know your students and your students to better know you. Early arrival encourages both on-time and early arrivals. More importantly, it fosters teacher-student relationships and a classroom team environment [as opposed to the too common adversarial environment].

- Given the specific text/course description/syllabus assigned, do you create a strategy and lesson plan that emphasizes/prioritizes this material in order of relevance in the 'real world'? As books and website texts tend to be increasingly longer, it is quite often impractical to expect the teacher to teach—and the students to learn—the totality of the material. Experience is usually the best reference for material prioritization. If a teacher [especially novice teachers] lacks a reasonable level of real-world experience, then the teacher could seek out assistance from more senior faculty both at the academic site and professionals in the field of interest. Network if you must! Consider the amount and level of material you never saw again in your educational journey. Inform your students that texts and website sources are great references. That said, remind your students that it is their responsibility to use both the written and website references. Remind your students that relevant references enable/enhance their knowledge base as well as the credibility of their educational efforts

- In a perfect world, all students for your class arrive equally and appropriately prepared for class. However, in the world in which we live , this is hardly the reality. As the course begins, do you make the effort to understand the students' backgrounds, i.e., academic requirements, strengths, weaknesses,...? Do you then strive to achieve some reasonable level of parity for the entire class? The class time to do this enables the entire class to move ahead at an increasingly greater pace with the passage of course time. A firm foundation is absolutely necessary; without it, the 'hole can only get deeper,' the 'slope is more slippery,' and the tendency to focus upon only the more capable students also creates the tendency to 'leave the other students further behind,' with their likelihood of a successful academic and knowledge outcome suffering accordingly.

- In a related matter, do you teach the course in a linear fashion, e.g., one topic/week through the course? In most courses—especially STEM courses—each chapter builds upon the preceding chapter/topic; consider moving ahead at a rate less than the linear rate during the earlier stages of the course in order to create that sound foundation that enables moving ahead at a rate increasingly greater than the average rate. Usual result: *a higher level of understanding for the students and, quite likely, time to address real-world examples.*

- Embedded in the above paragraph is the concept/principle of the 'comfort level' of the students; recall how you felt as a student in a class where the instructor was 'off to the races,' i.e., at an uncomfortable pace and/or style. The students' comfort level is a very important component within both the teaching style and the learning process as well as a strategy for efficient and effective classroom management. Consider those 'little things' that make your students more academically comfortable.

- Experience has abundantly demonstrated that the best classroom environment is one in which *both* the students and the teacher are learning. Experience has also shown that each student's question is, in fact, an excellent question and an opportunity for the student asking the question to learn and move forward. There are two related outcomes: [1] that same question is more than likely on the minds of most of the other students, and [2] the teacher's response to that question enables other students to ask questions. This opportunity fosters a 'team' perspective that includes both the students and the teacher. Conversely, students' questions should never be discouraged with denigrating comments, e.g., "You should already know that!" and other similar avoidance strategies employed by some teachers.

- Another lesson drawn from experience is that a student may pose a question that has never been asked before or anticipated. It's OK for the teacher to say, "That's an excellent question, but I don't know the answer. But I'll get the answer so that 'all of us' will know the answer, and thank you for asking that question!" Another great strategy that enhances the 'team' environment.

- The classroom is not an adversarial arena; it is not 'you' or 'me' but rather 'we'!

- Part of a team atmosphere is to encourage the formation of student teams during the lecture, laboratory, and problem-solving sessions. Perhaps some of the quiz/test taking could be the teams' efforts, much like the real world and professional atmosphere.

- Do you provide opportunities to demonstrate their levels of effort, e.g., extra credit assignments? Do you stress effort as one of the many ingredients to individual, team, academic, and professional success? Some teachers actually include a column for efforts in their traditional grade records. Within this column, the teacher records a '+ for effort' for each student's positive questions, comments, written assignments, tests, etc., which translates to extra credit added to their final course grade.

- Are you willing to conduct extra problem, reading and/or review sessions for the benefit of students in need of mentoring? One outcome is more efficient and effective classroom sessions.

- Are you aware that not all students respond equally to a particular teaching strategy? Creativity in teaching strategies is a useful resource; simply put, 'one size doesn't fit all.'

- Do you enable and encourage students' feedback? Students are an excellent barometer of 'what works' and 'what doesn't work.'

- Do you identify the goals of each class as well as the goals of the course? As an experienced teacher and mentor, I have frequently been asked, 'Why are we doing this?' So, let's tell them about the relevance and value of each topic. And if we don't know ourselves, let's find out so the entire class [students and teacher] are on the same page.

- Are your tests, exams, and assignments consistent with the material covered during class? There must be parity and relevance between teaching and testing.

- Do you integrate relevant Internet sources into your course? Do you use the internet to enable/encourage the students' awareness of material and developments beyond the textbook?

- Do you allow AI? What will your boundaries be?

- Do you strive to make your course 'pain-free'; this is not equivalent to 'work-free'? There is a difference!

- Do you use the students' evaluations as an opportunity for improvement?

- Do you privately and publicly encourage student feedback by welcoming their comments and criticisms that may improve the course for the students as well as the teacher?

And finally, the focus of this book has been on educating children living in challenging environments. The stresses of living create issues around toxic levels of cortisol. Brain damage related to cortisol, similar to the damage created by lead poisoning, impairs the executive functions of behavior/impulse controls—the major cause of disruptive classroom behaviors.

As also noted within other chapters, there is a natural antidote to toxic cortisol—nurturing. **Children crave nurturing.** Those who need it the most, the disruptive children, are often those who get it the least. Their behavior makes them unwelcome in the classroom. They are the ones most likely sent to the principal's office for "discipline." Ultimately, that discipline can lead to the "suspension to prison" slide.

One approach to this issue? Identify the child you, as the teacher, like the least—for whatever reason.

Say something positive to this child every day. As noted above, children crave nurturing. Over time, a child treated this way will come to school looking for that nurturing experience and, more importantly, not want to do anything to lose that nurturing. Such a child will be much more amenable to responding to requests to modify behaviors—such as, "Owen, sit down."

Discipline and punishment are not synonymous. Discipline is modifying behaviors. Punishment is one of the least effective ways of changing behaviors. **Positive relationships between teachers and students are the most effective means of replacing inappropriate behaviors with appropriate behaviors.** Nurturing is the key to creating those positive relationships.

As a side note, as this book was being written, this nation has experienced a number of school shootings. Invariably, the shooter is a male, former student looking to redress some former hurt created by the school. In some cases, it is bullying ; in others, suspensions and discipline. The most effective means of protecting students in schools has little to do with making school buildings "safer" and much to do with creating school environments that do not produce school shooters. Students who feel they have been nurtured and supported by their schools do not return to those schools with semiautomatic weapons.

CHAPTER 8

Educational Model: Linkage & Dynamics

> Learn to see. Realize that everything connects to everything else.
>
> —LEONARDI DA VINCI

> When everything is connected to everything else, *for better or worse,* everything matters!
>
> —BRUCE MAU

Introduction

THIS CHAPTER IS ESPECIALLY for visual learners! The preceding chapters of this book have each focused on a specific topic of educational relevance and interest for students, teachers, and families. This chapter—especially in the light of the two opening quotations—provides a 'systemic integration' of Chapters 1 -7. The reader may ask, "Why is this integration strategy necessary?" History is abundant with meaningful intentions and endeavors that are then less than perfect, as are their real-world results/performance, i.e., systems that fall short of their anticipated real-world performance. An important factor is that every system is composed of the 'parts/functions'.

That said, most efforts and systems have multiple parts. For example, a vehicle with one or more poor-performing parts will *never* perform as hoped for or anticipated. The purpose and motivation for this chapter are to provide a meaningful systemic, and inclusive educational model as a meaningful starting point for the analysis and improvement of those educational systems serving most—if not all—students with residence in the many strata of poverty.

The usefulness of such a model requires that each and all parts/functions are relevant to the *quantitative* metrics of educational success as opposed to those *qualitative* [and usually quite meaningless] metrics.

A car/vehicle with a part with a poor performing part, e.g., a flat tire or an overheated engine or lack of fuel, will never perform—as a system—as intended.

There exists a litany of outstanding research efforts throughout America—indeed, throughout the world—that focuses upon a single or limited scope of a 'piece' of the vast educational world. One must consider the relationships/linkages of all of the interrelated parts, i.e., their collective *'dynamics.'*

A prime example is the Hawthorne effect [R 8-1]. This phenomenon was found at a GE plant some years ago in the years 1924-1927. Time study engineers thought increasing lighting in a manufacturing area would improve production. They did, and it did. They increased the lighting further, and production continued to improve. To prove their hypothesis, they decided to see how much production would decrease with decreased lighting. They decreased lighting, and production still improved. Ultimately, it was determined the lighting had little or nothing to do with production levels. What was improving production was the attention being paid to workers while the experiments were going on!

Over that time span of three years, additional resources of time, budget, and resources were provided and expended with three successive

Illumination 'experiments.' The results were not consistent but rather contradictory. Although this experiment and its results are considered almost a century ago, there exists through that century since, many—in fact, too many—theories, trials, tests, and experiments that consume enormous levels of time, budget, and resources without a sustained successful level of performance. The common reason and rationale that analyses, experiments, and tests were conducted in limited test environments with little consideration for the realities of the 'real world.'

Figure 8-1 provides this book's framework and pathway. This particular model is research-based, experientially realistic, and inclusive as opposed to being *a limited representation/model.* This model evolved over four years of efforts by the three authors: a teacher and two individuals, each with multiple decades of research and educational experience. Their respective biographies are included in the Appendices.

Some observations of this Education Model: Linkages and Dynamics:

[1] Chapters 1-7 included several both forward and backward reflections providing some insight into the linkages and network dynamics embedded in Figure 8-1. For example, in the earlier chapters, the authors provided some forward reflections indicating that 'there is more to come' in a forthcoming chapter [or chapters]. On the other hand, in later chapters, the authors have referred the reader to statements in earlier chapters. These forward and backward reflections, i.e., the 'linkages,' reflect the 'dynamic' relationships' amongst the individual functions of Figure 8-1. This protocol now enables an awareness of the 'connectivity' of Chapters 1-7 and the forthcoming Chapters 9 and 10.

[2] *The linkage of this model serves to provide inputs to the process of teacher preparation.*

[3] In a similar fashion, the linkage between Chapters 2 and 3 also infers/ drives that the output of Chapter 2, Teacher Preparation, shapes the dynamics of 'teaching readiness' and, in some cases, 'teaching unreadiness.'

[4] However, the currently growing *'Teacher Shortage Crisis'* [cited in Chapter 2], with *greater* numbers of candidate teachers-to-be opting to pursue other professions *and more* teachers leaving the teaching profession, also impacts 'learning unreadiness' and 'teaching 'unreadiness' in Chapter 3 as well as creating a 'ripple factor' to learning readiness' and its 'enablers' and 'detractors' in Chapter 4.

[5] As we move on to Chapter 5, *Poverty in the Classroom: Family & Community Impact,* there is a growing awareness that each of these functions, independently and collectively, are not independent of each other but rather provide an increasing effect [aka this 'rippling factor'] as the readers migrate through the *functional education model.*

[6] That said, the reader moves on to Chapter 6, *Classroom Environment* and the classroom realities influenced by the inequities of teacher preparation, teacher shortages, 'teaching readiness,' 'teaching unreadiness,' and the effects of 'poverty in the classroom,' family, and community .

[7] *The readers are invited to consider the individual and collective impacts of this functional education model and, then, the positive impacts offered by Chapter 7, Classroom Management & Teacher Leadership,* and *Chapter 9, Roles of Advocacy, Support, and Mentoring for the Teachers in the Classroom...and their Students and their Families.*

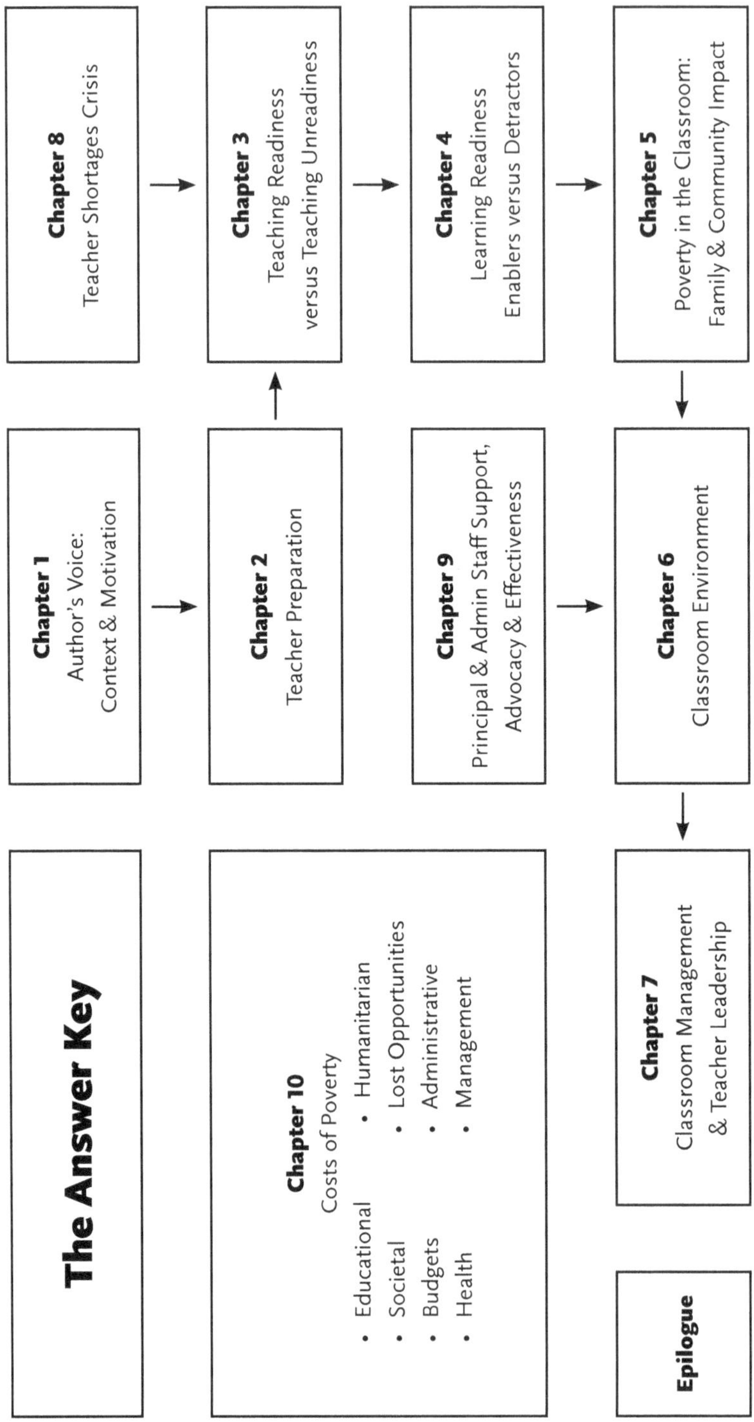

Figure 8-1 *Functional Education Model: Linkages and Dynamics*

[8] The authors respectfully encourage the readers to take advantage of the abundance of reference books that address [1] Simulation Modeling and Analysis and [2] Systems Analysis and Synthesis; both are, historically, tools and skills that are necessary and sufficient for systems design! That said, the reader is now asked to consider the overall impact of the totality of the network 'linkages' and 'dynamics' of this functional educational model.

[9] Consider Chapter 10; there exists a litany of 'costs' associated with the effects of poverty. Beyond the steadily increasing 'dollar costs,' the starting list of costs includes societal, educational, health, budgets, planning, humanitarian, 'lost opportunities', administrative, management, and justice system inequities. *The constantly increasing totality of these costs , historically, continues to increase the gap between available budgetary resources and the constantly increasing totality of the cited costs.*

[10] The closing message of Chapter 10 considers two options:

1. Continue the current trend cited in Figure 10-1 [aka 'business as usual'] or
2. Connecting the 'dots' that suggest the opportunity cited in Figure 8-1.

[11] The three authors also respectfully encourage readers to read and ponder the Chapter 8 opening quotes of Leonardi Da Vinci and Bruce Mau again.

[12] For all the students, teachers-to-be, teachers, parents, and mentors:

Don't just learn, experience.

Don't just read, absorb.

Don't just change, transform.

Don't just relate, advocate.
Don't just promise, prove.
Don't just criticize, encourage.
Don't just think, ponder.
Don't just take, give
Don't just see, feel.
Don't just dream, do.
Don't just hear, listen.
Don't just talk, act.
Don't just tell, show.
Don't just exist, live.

—ROY T. BENNETT, *THE LIGHT IN THE HEART* [R 8-2]

Finally, the latter of the two opening quotations of this chapter may now take on a greater educational meaning:

> Everything is connected to everything else, for better or worse, everything matters!
>
> —BRUCE MAU

CHAPTER 9

The Value of Mentoring for Children Living in Poverty

> The best mentoring for those with the greatest need comes from within...from the heart and the mind!
>
> —UNKNOWN

Primer for This Chapter

- Referring to the above quotation, the authors believe it is their responsibility to remind the readers that, for the most part, the children of poverty do not experience the full benefits of mentoring. Conversely, that mentoring so readily available to children having the resources to provide significant educational supports that complement and supplement in-school education exists!
- The genesis for a *PRIMER on* mentoring is cited in Chapter 2, *TEACHER PREPARATION!*, e.g., in [R 2-4] and [R 2-6]. From [R 2-4]:
    - Preparing prospective teachers to meet the challenges of working with higher-need students.
    - Differentiating instruction based on individual student needs.

    - Understanding how a student's culture and economic status impact how they learn.
- The value of mentoring is not limited to students. From [R 2-4]:

    > Do college faculty continue to work with newly certified teachers once they secure a teaching job, or does their mentoring end once they leave the teacher preparation programs? Do schools provide mentoring for new teachers, particularly in schools serving the neediest students?

- "Create a team of mentors who work with the next generation of principals and other school leaders." [R 2-6]. School administrators, particularly new administrators, would benefit from mentoring.
- And, whenever and wherever possible, children living in poverty would benefit greatly if their parents received support (mentoring).

Background/Synopsis

- *Let's Start with the Children [R 9-1]* Book #1 of what has become a trilogy :

    > The sixteen-year ministry with families and children in the South Bronx provided the opportunity to raise some relevant societal questions, e.g., Why is there so much sustained poverty? Why are the children of poverty seemingly being denied a meaningful education?

- *Poverty & Despair versus Education & Opportunity [9-2a].* From Book #2 of this trilogy:

    > Poverty and its lifelong impact on the quality of life, health, and opportunity for those living in poverty.

- *Poverty, Not Schools, To Blame for Low Scores [9-2b],* Joseph H. Crowley, *OPINION,* Providence Journal, November 27, 2015.
    - From this Book #3 of the trilogy:

    > Specific attention is paid to the poverty-education linkage and dynamics that have led to millions of children reaching the schoolhouse door already years behind their wealthier

peers, i.e., the learning gaps. The conditions that create this imbalance persist throughout a child's time in school as long as the child lives in a poverty environment. Unfortunately, closing the learning gaps during a normal school day and year has been an exercise in futility. According to the National Assessment of Educational Progress, all of the time and funds provided for No Child Left Behind and its successor programs have had no impact whatsoever on closing the learning gaps.

Mentoring Enables a Meaningful Education

Mentoring is sharing knowledge, skills, experience, support, advocacy, and even 'hope' with others in dire need of mentoring. The goal is to provide a role model, guidance, encouragement, and relevant insights to motivate the mentees to achieve their fullest potential.

This chapter is intended to stress the benefits of mentorship. Google provides an almost endless amount of information concerning the purpose and benefits of mentoring. The benefits are well recognized. The growth of people in business, politics, the military, medicine, and numerous others—including educational arenas and a spectrum of endeavors, large and small, is enhanced via mentoring protocols.

Authors Crowley and Colella had multiple career opportunities to be mentoring advocates. A representative example is a mentoring program for newly-to-be-graduated engineering students. The previous practice had been to provide the students with reams of relevant reading materials but provided no guidance in terms of which materials would be most beneficial nor which materials pertained to the various aspects of their new careers.

The new mentoring program provided incoming graduates with an individual experience in what the novices would be experiencing. Mentoring minimized the learning curves for the newcomers, saving considerable dollars in bringing the new employees up to productivity standards. The camaraderie developed in the mentoring program was evident in the improved esprit de corps throughout the organization.

Resources for those of you who would like to know more about the specifics of mentoring for your students include the following references for practical information on gaining the benefits of mentoring for your students: Google Search process [R 9-3].

If your school is not currently taking advantage of available mentoring resources, you might ask the administration to look into the many literacy mentoring programs, such as the Literacy Volunteers of America [LVA] and the Child Literacy Program in America serving children through the 6th grade. References [[R 9-4], [R 9-5], [R 9-6], [R 9-7] are especially representative and helpful for an added insight into the mentoring process. Look to the following references for after-school and summer literacy programs [R 9-8]. Another example is the Innovative Approaches to Literacy [IAL] [R 9-9], which supports high-quality programs for developing literacy skills for children from birth through the 12th grade.

Authors (Crowley & Colella) each have experience with five decades of mentoring—much of it at high school, college levels, and a variety of inner-city programs. However, one of the more exemplary experiences has been with the San Miguel [Middle] School serving inner-city students from the Providence urban ring.

Each student in the school is provided with a mentor. Mentors are encouraged to continue their life mentoring as their mentees progress through high school and beyond. The school is always open to graduates who may need support and, a very rewarding side note, former students who return to help other students.

Remembering the students are all from homes suffering from poverty ; their academic success rate is applaudable. Graduating from San Miguel in the eighth grade, they are accepted into many of the area's most competitive high schools. While the average graduation rate for Rhode Island hovers around 85%, and the graduation rate for low SES students is lower, 97.5% of San Miguel students graduate from high school.

The San Miguel program is exemplary in terms of maximizing the potential of mentoring. The program requires a large staff and community support commitment to maintain its success in educating students living in poverty. What it does do is prove the value of mentoring to that target population of students. It is recognized that successful mentoring at San Miguel is a meaningful reference/goal for the cooperation of the students and parents or guardians of these middle-school students. You can also contact local organizations such as Big Brothers/ Big Sisters and Literacy Volunteers of America for volunteers. Schools having a public service requirement for graduation have many students who would, themselves, benefit from providing mentoring and tutoring services to needy children.

A Google search will provide vast amounts of resources to assist you in coordinating and monitoring mentor relationships (there are additional relevant mentoring references in the *REFERENCES APPENDIX* [Chapter 9] of this book). If you do take the challenge, target your neediest students. You will gain first-hand knowledge of the benefits of mentoring when you observe the difference between the students fortunate enough to have mentors and those who do not.

Revisiting the Message of This Book

The population of concern and need addressed in the chapters of this book are those children and their families surviving within the various strata of poverty. The authors' concentration is the life-long educational and other inequities that limit the lives and opportunities of countless children living in poverty generation after generation. Living in poverty is stressful. The humanitarian costs far outweigh the dollar costs.

To reiterate, mentoring has significant benefits within the educational arena. We first stress the need for mentors for students. However, mentoring for new and struggling teachers—particularly those serving our neediest students—is equally important. Nationally, there is a shortage of school administrators, meaning, if it can be done, a large number of new administrators would also benefit from, if not require, mentoring. And finally, there are the parents, most of whom are doing the best they can to raise and support their children but would benefit from some helping hands.

> The King will reply, "Truly I tell you, whatever you did for one of the least of these brothers and sisters of mine, you did for me."
>
> —MATTHEW 25:40,
> NEW INTERNATIONAL VERSES [NIV]

CHAPTER 10

The Collective Poverty + Educational Costs

> Poverty, not schools, to blame for low scores.
>
> —JOSEPH H. CROWLEY [R 10-1]
>
> The road out of poverty still runs past the schoolhouse door.
>
> —DREW SNYDER [R 10-2]

The necessary preamble for this chapter is the 'Social Sciences/Education' reminder found on the rear book cover of R 10-3 [Book #2 of Trilogy]. It follows next on pages 2 and 3.

Introduction

FIRST, IT MUST BE SAID that the term 'costs' is multi-dimensional! 'Costs' include the loss of the student's learning readiness and, in some cases, the teachers' teaching readiness and the cost of an unmeaningful education, the continuing historical loss of opportunity for so many students, social costs, steadily increasing budgets, health, humanitarian, justice inequalities and incarceration costs, and most importantly, opting for 'business as usual' rather than [a] enabling the outstanding requirements for enabling learning readiness for those students in need and [b]'cost reductions' across this, currently, unacceptable cost spectrum.

In 2016, Colella & Crowley [R 10-3] provided an early message concerning the linkage between those readiness factors [p. 80] that enable a productive life. Conversely, they also provided the linkage between the *lack of 'readiness'* and a spectrum of 'inequalities' [p. 82]. Most importantly, they also provided the linkage between *educational readiness factors* and the spectrum of *poverty-driven inequalities!*

[R 10-3] also includes *Appendix C: Life Cycle Costs-What are they? A necessary part of the solution? [pp. 134-141]*

https://www.poverty-inequalities [R 10-4] is an important and relevant companion reference for [R 10-3] with its abundance of references!

The intention of this book is to prepare *teachers-to-be and active* teachers to appropriately respond to the educational needs of children growing up in poverty and its life-long disadvantages and educational disabilities. It is readily apparent from previous research-based chapters that the circumstances of living in poverty create serious impediments to learning. There are two aspects to these impediments.

The first is the impact of living a very stressful life , i.e., that litany of poverty-induced stresses. For the young child, the stresses, both in duration and intensity, produce toxic levels of cortisol. The amygdala, hippocampus, and prefrontal cortex do not develop normally. Toxic cortisol leads to impaired concentration and short-term memory—two critical components of classroom success. That said, keeping such a child on task takes a herculean effort on the part of the teacher.

The second issue, also cortisol-related, is the brain's executive function does not develop properly, resulting in impaired behavior and impulse control. This last characteristic of teaching children growing up in a highly stressful, limited educational support environment is the main focus of this book [R 10-4].

Being day-to-day in the classroom, a teacher may not think about the long-term consequences of today's vocabulary words or multiplication exercises. Less still, the impact on a child of the positive and negative interactions between the child and teacher. As one poster quotes, "They may forget what you said, but they will not forget how you made them feel." [R 10-5]

An Edutopia article (Feb. 4, 2019) [R 10-6] speaks to the influence good teachers have on students that goes far beyond achievement test scores. In one study, ninth-grade teachers who improved students' motivation, ability to adapt to new situations, and self-regulation set students on a path of better attendance, fewer suspensions, and higher graduate rates.

Although the intent of this book is not to teach economics, having a better understanding of the long-term economic and other benefits children derive from their interactions with teachers might be just the push one needs to step back into a challenging classroom.

What exactly is it that a school accomplishes? Especially one with good teachers. We can start with Pre-K programs. On the surface, pre-K orients a child to school and teaches some basic skills like the alphabet, numbers, shapes, and colors. What about the long term? One study by the National Institute for Early Education Research [R 10-7] suggests that for every $1 invested in quality pre-K programs, there is a return on investment of $17 in social benefits.

But the benefits go well beyond earning power. As noted in other chapters, children living in poverty are exposed to stresses which produce toxic levels of cortisol. Toxic cortisol not only damages the developing brain but is an inflammatory affecting all of a child's organs. The one natural antidote to toxic cortisol is nurturing. Removing a three or four -year-old child from a stressful, toxic environment to a year in a nurturing, supportive school environment has some profound long-term benefits.

The U.S. Department of Justice [R 10-8] reports children provided Pre-K classes have increased emotional and cognitive development, improved child/parent relationships, and fewer instances of child abuse as children and drug abuse as adults. In the long term, both parents and child develop increased economic self-sufficiency (a side benefit of Pre-K programs is the childcare aspect, which allows parents to work more with fewer child care expenses). The cortisol-created damage to the brain's executive function and behavior/impulse control cannot be understated. Other studies have found children who attend Pre-K programs have, over time, a 25% lower rate of incarcerations and violent crimes.

Moving to the other end of the spectrum, what would be the impact of increasing the national high school graduation rate ? Can you identify one child, particularly a child living in poverty with little support for education, who is destined to drop out of school but, with your support and encouragement, might see that graduation stage? A report from the America's Promise Alliance [R 10-9] suggests moving our current national graduation rate from roughly 85% to 90%, about 250,000 more graduates nationwide, would provide significant rewards. Earnings would increase by $3.1 billion and tax income by $664 million. Economic growth would go up by $5.7 billion, and 14,260 new jobs would be created. A surprising savings of $16.1 billion in health care costs is also predicted. As noted above, mitigation of the effects of toxic cortisol has a dramatic impact on incarcerations. Prisons and jails in the United States cost over $80 billion per year. According to a Stanford study, 68% of males in prison do not have a high school diploma. The success of our schools and our students has a profound impact on the economic and social well-being of all Americans.

And what of the time between Pre-K and graduation—your time with students? If all students were to achieve basic mastery, by National Assessment of Educational Progress (NAEP) standards, America's Gross Disposable Product (GDP) would increase by $32 trillion—yes, $32,000,000,000,000!

Dana Mitra, Associate Professor of Education at Pennsylvania State University in Social Benefits of Public Education [R 10-10], provides a list of benefits associated with public education. Some of the report's findings:

- In comparison to graduates, high school dropouts have twice the unemployment rate and are three times more likely to receive welfare.
- Cutting drop out rates by half would generate $45B in net economic benefit.
- Twice as many inmates lack diplomas as the general adult population , and the annual cost of incarceration is almost three times the cost of one year's education.
- Increasing the male graduation rate by 5% would save $5B in crime-related expenses (prisons, jails, and the other facets of the criminal justice system).
- Each year of schooling decreases the mortality rate for men by 7.2% and 6% for women.
- Dropouts cost $2700 per year in public health programs; if every student in a single year graduated, national health care costs would be reduced by $40B.
- A high school diploma reduces the rate of alcohol abuse by six times.
- If the median education level rose by one year, there would be 13% more voters in political primaries.

You play two roles in this as a professional educator. As noted above, every child you can support—to the extent that the child graduates from high school—has an impact on our national economy. On a more singular, humane level, every child you help to cross the stage at graduation will have less chance of raising a family in poverty, will be more financially secure, will be healthier both physically and mentally, and will have much less chance of being negatively involved in the criminal justice system.

The second role you can play as a professional educator is one too few educators involve themselves in. Some of the economic and social benefits of a good education are listed above. There are reams and reams of research supporting the notion that dollars spent on education are an investment—not a cost. There is a certain irony at the sight of parents at a town financial meeting fighting to keep their taxes down by not spending on schools and then turning around and writing $50,000 or $60,000 checks for college tuition. They cannot seem to draw the connection between the foundation needed for college, as provided by their elementary and secondary schools, and a student's success in college courses.

You can publicly promote the funding of our public schools. There are those who will argue you are simply feathering your own nest. More importantly, you are looking to feather the nests all of our children must pass through our public education system.

One last point. As noted throughout these chapters, eliminating the so-called learning gaps between richer and poorer students should be a national goal.

Previous efforts, fostered by the false assumptions underlying No Child Left Behind, have all failed. Some not only failed but made learning worse for children living in poverty. Efforts to improve test scores of needy children by reducing their curriculum to only subjects being tested was a travesty. Students most in need of a broad education, including art and music, were denied in an effort to save teachers jobs by reducing the differences in test scores. In reading through research, the one effective way to level the playing field between students in diverse socioeconomic circumstances is to provide more school time for our neediest students. One bright light for these children is proposals for universal preschool programs. The programs will be a boon for children living in poverty but will not be if all children, rich and poor, are provided access to the programs. Learning levels, as measured by standardized tests, will continue to exist if needy children are not given more schooling than their wealthier peers.

This chapter speaks about the national impact of students not graduating from high school: Trillions of dollars in lost economic opportunity, more in excess health costs, and billions in social support services required by those ill-equipped to care for themselves and their families.

Add to that the billions of dollars in costs for our prisons and legal system that might be averted by simply reducing our numbers of school 'drop-outs.' You might ask, I'm just one teacher; what difference can I make?

That question leads to another asked of a child. A storm had driven thousands and thousands of starfish onto the shore. A child was walking along, picking up starfish and tossing them back into the ocean. An adult happened by and noticed the child. The adult asked the child, "There are thousands and thousands of starfish on this beach . What difference do you think you are making?" As the child picked up another starfish and tossed it into the water, the child responded, "I'm making a difference for that one." If you only make a difference for one child, you are making a difference.

You are an educator. You need not limit your educational power to the classroom. You can be an advocate for your students, your school, and our public education system. Whenever given the opportunity, at a cocktail party, Rotary meeting, or with a letter to the local paper, be an advocate for America's public education system. It is what made this country a world power and what is needed to keep it as a world power!

Business As Usual?... Connecting the Dots?... Or Opportunity?

Business As Usual

Within the context of this book and the population of educationally disadvantaged students, Figure 10-1* [next page] reflects [1] the constantly *increasing* annual costs in billions of America's public school systems and [2] its companion: the constantly increasing inequities experienced by children of poverty. Another way of saying the same 'truths' are [1] unacceptable and clearly untenable and [2] a continuing disservice to the children of poverty . This situation is costly in so many ways and is represented by {1} the constantly unacceptable rising costs of {TC/SQ}, i.e., the Total Dollar Costs of the Status Quo Policy—aka the 'do-nothing-different-policy'—and {2} the constantly increasing

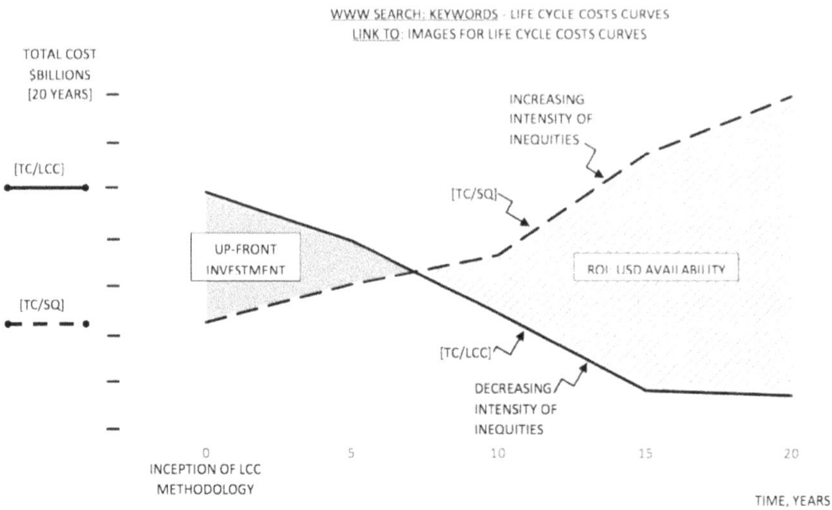

FIGURE C-1 - TOTAL [TC/SQ] AND [TC/LCC] PROFILES

number and intensity of inequities experienced by the innocent children of poverty! These *tangible costs, i.e., __________;* however, the so often *less considered intangible costs and indirect costs* go well beyond the budget $$. The spectrum of these latter costs includes degradation of the overall quality of life for those living in poverty, degradation of the humanity of those living in poverty, loss of educational opportunities, loss of employment, loss of upward mobility, compromised health, family instability, addiction, abuse, violence in the homes and on the street, incarceration, recidivism, an uneven playing field in the stadiums of civil and criminal justice et al. These intangible and indirect costs do have a huge price tag in dollars!

*Supportive data is available in [R 10-4], Section C, *COSTS.*

Connecting the Dots

It is difficult to 'connect the dots' by annual performance assessments of the public school systems servicing children in poverty! Historically, as annual costs increase, so does the chaotic administration and management of most public schools that reside in areas of poverty;

from the residence in poverty, its disadvantages & life-long disabilities, learning & teaching *unreadiness* factors, short-range, increasing and unacceptable spectrum of costs, educational disservice for children [millions], continuing issue of short-range educational projections, limited acknowledgment of 'what could be' and more. Simply put, poverty is a multi-edged sword that is the major roadblock along the many roads that *could but do not go to the schoolhouse doors!*

Before addressing 'opportunity,' it is important to provide a summary of the *COMMENTARY* [R 10-11] by Joseph H. Crowley, a former president of the Rhode Island Association of School Principals and a respected and recognized educational consultant. He is also a respected researcher on public school education and its successes for many students and its long-standing failures to lift up the children of poverty via a meaningful education so readily available to those students in residence beyond the virtual walls of poverty! His commentary is entitled *'Don't just spend-invest in RI's children.'* A summary follows:

- The differences in standard test scores between more and dramatically less affluent children have been consistently addressed by Mr. Crowley.
- The financial benefits of getting more children to a high school diploma are enormous; studies suggest a $7 return for every dollar spent for pre-K.
- Also, the child-care benefit of pre-K would yield more than $8 billion per year nationally in parent earnings.
- Pre-K participants have a 45% lower rate of incarceration and are involved in 1/3 fewer violent crimes,
- American's prisons and jails cost $8 billion/year.
- Pre-K participants are 25% less likely to receive government assistance.
- Government assistance programs cost over $750 billion; a simple 1% reduction in these costs is $7,580,000,000,

- Getting more students to graduate from high school has similar benefits.

  Clearly, simply getting students over the hurdle of a high school diploma has a huge economic impact.
- These are our concentrations of students living in poverty and needing additional education support. Let us *invest* in longer school days and/or school years for these schools.
- Sadly, America has had one of the highest rates of childhood poverty in the developed countries. *There is a direct inverse correlation between education and poverty.*

  Also of equal importance is the linkage between the areas of 'Up-Front Investment' and the multiple ROI [Return on Investment]. These factors focus on the fiscal benefits via USD Availability that enable raising children out of poverty. Investments in education will also move many Americans out of the lifelong miserable circumstances poverty creates. *It is only the most fiscally prudent and humanitarian thing to do!*

Opportunity

Figure 10-2 [next page] provides [1] the sustained benefits/advantages of considering *educational budgets + 'investment resources' as an educational investment.* This educational *investment, initially, is an added but decreasing cost over time* and [2] also of significant importance, decreasing educational inequalities over time. and [3] additional ROI/resources to provide the outstanding need for students' learning readiness, teaching readiness, school facilities, mentors, administrative and family active advocacy and support., i.e., enabling educational highways that do go to and through the doors of all the public schools! Figure 10-2 offers a view of the future excerpt from Figure 10-1

Some added insight from https://www.poverty-inequalities.com follows:

NOTE: Figure 10-2 provides the hope for the future!

Return on Investment [ROI] has its origin in dollar profitability with

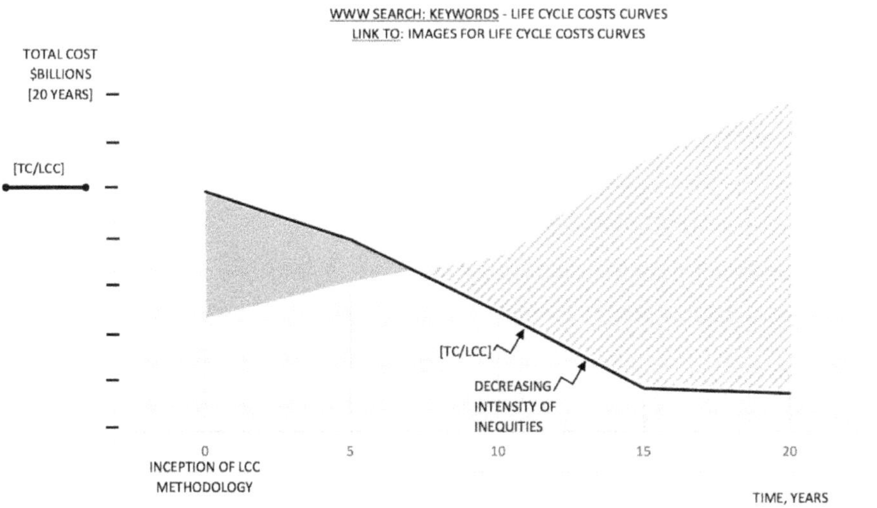

FIGURE C-2 - A LONG TERM VIEW OF THE OUTCOME TRENDS OF THE ELIMINATION OF POVERTY

respect to investment [dollars]. ROI has been, is, and shall always be an important consideration for the *goal-driven* expenditure/consumption of resources. In the financial arena, dollars are the capital of interest. In the business arenas, growth, stability, 'brand' market share, etc., as well as dollars, together. Constitute the capital of interest. The capital of interest within *Poverty & Despair versus Education & Opportunity* [R 10-4] is the quality of life and a level 'playing field' of [educational] opportunity, justice, and humanitarian efforts for all, especially for those living in poverty for reasons and causes beyond their control... *and...* the goal of providing a road out of poverty and the freedom from poverty- driven inequalities!

> Perhaps the most valuable result of all education is the ability to make yourself do the thing you have to do, when it ought to be done, whether you like it or not; it is the first lesson that ought to be learned; and however early a man's training begins, it is probably the last lesson that he learns thoroughly.

—TECHNICAL EDUCATION [1877]

> Education is the most powerful weapon which you can use to change the world.
>
> —NELSON MANDELA

Authors' note: Chapter 10 closes with Figure 10-2 that, for the children of poverty, will clearly demonstrate the dramatic difference between 'business as usual' [see Figure 10-1] and the 'educational and ROI-enabled opportunity that can be realized.' Figure 10-1 clearly reflects the enormous and continuing spectrum of unacceptable/untenable cost increases, and the model for Figure 10-2 is the updated version of p. 140 [R 10-3]: *Poverty & Despair vs. Education & Opportunity.*

Epilogue

WE, YOU AND I, have combed through these chapters, research, and experiences. You are probably overwhelmed with thoughts and feelings, at least one of which, I am sure, is heartbreak. I share that I am personally heartbroken when I think about our system as we have and know it in 2023. Many of us out in the educational trenches are trying and working tirelessly to keep the system's shortcomings from affecting our students. And it is exhausting!

We—my grandfather, Joseph Crowley, and I—write this to validate your thoughts and feelings or possibly help you identify what has been hovering in the back of your mind. I sincerely hope that the chapters of this book provide some guidance or light on how to connect the dots with respect to why teaching is so hard. It was guidance and validation that I knew I needed after a long and trying day.

As you move forward, I respectfully ask that you think back to find your why.

If you haven't heard this before, let me quickly explain: our 'why' is the reason we stepped into this field of education. Did you opt to join the teacher ranks because of your love of learning and teaching? Your enjoyment at enabling and watching children make connections? Supporting them as the next generation is formed into the citizens of tomorrow as they go into the world? I share mine with the hope that it will spark your thoughts and reflections.

My 'why' is to help and enable students : those who both fall through the cracks because they 'fly below the radar' and those whose challenges makes their school experience more complex. I believe that all students need an advocate and, if that cannot be or not, a 'caregiver.' I feel that it is the teacher's responsibility to advocate for the student's best interests. Now, as you can imagine, that can lead to long hours, sleepless nights, and stressful days, but it does comfort me [now] to reflect and acknowledge that I always did the best I could with the resources and support available to me at that time.

I am well aware that we have used the word 'hope' frequently in this book, and it is possibly exhausting, but nevertheless, I do 'hope' that this book provides you with that!

Hope that the knowledge is out there!

Hope that the system can be upgraded to better serve those teachers and students tangled up in it!

And I hope that you, your colleagues, your family, are doing your best, even though it is difficult and could feel as if you are not making a difference in the processes of learning and teaching or that outside factors gave you the impression that you are the 'problem'!

I leave you with these closing thoughts as I imagine sitting across the table from you:

Your feelings are valid!

You are [I hope] continuing to do your best!
You are making a difference!

This is where we part, my colleagues & friends.
Onward and upward! Go change the world!

—Kimberly Deninger

APPENDIX

Chapter References

Chapter 1: Author's Voice, Context & Motivation

R1-1 Parenting Matters Conference, Bradley Hospital, the nation's first psychiatric hospital for children, and Lifespan Community Health Institute present the 32nd Parenting Matters Conference as a virtual event via [Zoom]. This half=day event offers parents, childcare providers, social workers and teachers a unique opportunity to learn from top child development and behavior professionals in a casual setting.

R 1-2 Parenting Matters. Supporting Parents of Children 0-8, National Academies of Sciences, Engineering and Medicine; Division of Behavioral and Social Sciences and Education; Board on Children, Youth and Families; Committee on Supporting the Parents of Young Children; Editors: Heather Brenner, Morgan Ford and Vivian L. Gadsden, November 21, 2016.

R 1-3 Slap A Teacher Challenge, TIK TOK, 2021.

Chapter 2: Teacher Preparation

R 2-1 Improved Education! Listen to the Teachers, *YOUR TURN,* Barbara A. Vanvillas, Guest Columnist, Providence Journal, November 17, 2021.

R 2-2 How to Support Multilingual Learners with Higher Expectations, Suzanne arks, TNTP BLOG, March 28, 2022.

R 2-3 Articles by James A. Kadamus, Newsletter, Times Union [Albany], Las Vegas Sun, Providence Journal, Inside Sources.

R 2-4 Poor Teacher Preparation in R.I., James A. Kadamus and Joseph P. Frey, *OPINION,* Providence Journal, October 1, 2019

R 2-5 Five Key Steps to Fixing R.I. Schools, James A. Kadamus, *MY VIEW,* Providence Journal, September 1, 2019.

R 2-6 Strategies to Fix Providence's Failing School, James A. Kadamus, *MY TURN,* Providence Journal, March 1, 2020.

R 2-7 R.I.'s Chance to Remake Schools, Ron Wolk, Providence Journal, April 28, 2015.

R 2-8 Poverty & Despair vs. Education & Opportunity, Joseph H. Crowley, and Albert M. Colella [PhD], Stillwater Publications, 2016.

R 2-9 https://www.poverty-inequalities.com

R 2-10 Providence Schools are structured to fail, Julia Steiny, *OPINION,* Providence Journal, April11, 2022.

R 2-11 Making Good Humans, Getting Parents Aboard, Teryn Bong-Clegg, September 15, 2018.

R 2-12 Graduates are still not ready, James A. Kadamus, Providence Journal, October 11, 2017.

R 2-13 We need to teach teachers better, James A. Kadamus, Providence Journal, January 1, 2016.

R 2-14 Dr. Rimm-Kaufman, Commonwealth Professor of Education, School of Education and Human Development, University of Virginia, serk@virginia.edu.

R 2-15 Not Enough Teachers, The Week Staff, August 28, 2022.

R 2-15a KIDS COUNT REPORT, Providence Journal, May 15, 2023.

R 2-16 4 Strategies To Increase Teacher Retention, Hanover Research, Worldwide ERC, 4401 Wilson Blvd #4th , Virginia, VA 22203.

R 2-17 Understanding Teacher Shortages: 2018 Update, Learning Policy Institute, A State-by-State Analysis of the Factors Influencing Teacher Supply, Demand and Equity, August 24, 2018.

R 2-18 Are Teacher Shortages Worse Than We Thought?, Education Week, 2019.

R 2-19 The Teacher Shortage is Real, Large and Growing and Worse Than We Thought, Economic Policy Institute [EPI], Emma Garcia, Elaine Weiss, March 26, 219.

R 2-20 "It's Harder Than Ever": What We've Been Hearing About Teacher Shortages, TNTP, Bailey Cato Czupruk, Match 3, 2022.

R 2-21 These 4 Strategies Can Help Schools Retain Their Best Teachers, Victoria Van Cleef. TNTP BLOG, May 12, 2022.

R 2-22 How a 30-Second Survey Can Help Schools Retain Teachers, TNTP BLOG, Kevin Haynes April7, 2022.

R 2-23 Best Elementary Teacher Education Programs, https://www.usnews.com/best-graduate-scholarship-education-schools/teachers-education-rankings, 2021.

R 2-24 Teacher Education Programs in America, Schools in the USA.com, https://www.schoolsintheusa.com/TeacherEducationPrograms.cfm.

R 2-25 Brave Teacher Gave Me Courage, Chris Fortunato, MY TURN, Providence Journal, May 8,2018.

R 2-26 DEANS for IMPACT, Williams-Black How, Fueling the fire of teaching desire. How tutoring is helping one future teacher, March 2022.

R 2-27 LEANLAB EDUCATION: https:www. leanlabeducation.org.

R 2-28 Workplace Skills, Google, LINCS.

R 2-29 Autism Spectrum Disorder: 498 [1993-1994] to 31,193 [2015-2016].

Chapter 3: Teaching Readiness versus Teaching Unreadiness

R 3-1 A Framework For Understanding Poverty, Ruby K. Payne, PhD, 4th Revised Edition, aha! Process Inc., 2005.

R 3-2 Poverty & Despair versus Education & Opportunity, J. Crowley, A. Colella, Stillwater River Publications, 2016.

R 3-3 Protective Factors for School Readiness Among Children in Poverty, Matthew R. Holiday, Adriana Cimetta, Christina A. Cutshaw, David Yaden & Ronald W. Marx, Journal of Education for Students Placed at Risk [JESPAR], Pages 125-147, Volume 19, 2014.

R 3-4 "All" Doesn't Work in Education, Sarah Mead, Blog, Whitby School, Greenwich, CT.

R 3-5 Adverse Childhood Experience [ACE], How Children Succeed, Paul Tough, Houghton Mifflin Harcourt, 2012.

R 3-6 'One Size Doesn't Fit All', Allison Sherman, Center for Positive Organizations, July 25, 2014.

R 3-7 When 'One Size Doesn't Fit All', Mina Freeburg, Student Vooice, October 9, 2014.

R 3-8 The Elements of Teaching, James M. Banner, Jr., Harold C Cannon, Yale University Press, 1997.

R 3-9 The Progressive Teacher, P. Ajtitha, http://www.progressive teacher.in/teacher/readiness.

R 3-10 5 Elements Needed To Build Motivation, Resilience and Career Readiness in Your Students, Matthew Lynch, The Advocate, April 8, 2019.

R 3-11 Ten Books That Can Revolutionize Teaching Practice, Anne Rubin, We Are Teachers, March 7, 2019.

R 3-12Novice Teacher Perceptions of the Soft Skills Needed in Today's Workplace, Tang Keow Ngang, Nor Hashimah, Hashimah Mohd Yunus, Procedia Social and Behavioral Sciences, also GLOBE-EDU, July 14, 2014.

R 3-13 Tomorrow's Teachers, The Holmes Group Notes, Rebecca West Burns, 1986.

R 3-14a Poverty, Not Schools, To Blame For Low Scores, Joseph H. Crowley, *OPINION,* Providence Journal, November 27, 2015.

R 3-14b Making All Schoolchildren Winners, Joseph H. *Crowley, OPINION,* Providence Journal, February 7, 2021.

R 3-15 We Need To Teach Teachers Better, John J. Colby, *OPINION,* Providence Journal, January 1, 2016.

R 3-16 *Poor Teacher Preparation in R.I., James A. Kadamus, Joseph P.* Frey, *OUR TURN,* Providence Journal, November 1, 2019.

Chapter 4: Learning Readiness: Enablers versus Detractors

R 4-1 Determinants of Teaching & Learning, Susan B. Bastable, Sharon Kitchie, Chapter 4, 2nd Edition, Jones & Bartlett Publishers, Inc., 2003.

R 4-2 Social Promotions, Pros and Cons, Brandon Gaille, July 7, 2015.

R 4-3 Poverty, Not Schools, To Blame For Low Scores, Joseph H. Crowley, *OPINION,* Providence Journal, November 27, 2015.

R 4-4 Let's Start with the Children, Colella, A. Lippincott, S., Westbow Press, 2013.

R 4-5 Socioeconomic Status and Education, Google, e.g. Cutting Class, Edited by Kincheloe, J., Steinberg, S.R., Rowman & Littlefield Publishers, Inc. New York, 2007.

R 4-6 U.S. Poverty rises despite economic recovery, Economy, reporting by Lucia Mulikani, Caroline Hurner and Susan Heavy, edited by Mohammed Zargam, September 17, 2013.

R 4-7 National Center of Children n Poverty, [NCCP], Mailman School of Public Health, Columbia University.

R 4-8 Education Week, Standards-based Accountability's High Stakes, R. Wolk, November 8, 2008.

R 4-9 It's All About Education: How Poverty Impacts Brain Development and Learning, Laura Lee, GotLocalProvEducation Expert, April 29, 2015.

R 4-10 Adverse Childhood Experiences [ACE], How Children Succeed, Paul Tough, Houghton Mifflin Harcourt, 1023.

R 4-11 Chasing the Dream: Poverty and Opportunity in America, Dr. Kimberly Noble, Metrofocus, June 23, 2015.

R 4-12 Protecting Children from Toxic Stress, David Bornstein, The Opinion Pages, New York Times, June 23, 2015.

R 4-13 The High Moral and Economic Cost of Poverty in America, Marion Wright Edelman, Child Watch Column, Children's Defense Fund, September 19, 2014.

R 4-14 The Economic Impact of the Achievement Gap in America's schools, McKinsey & Company, Social Studies Office, April, 2009.

R 4-15 The effects of Poverty on Childhood Brain Development. Joan Luby, Andy Belden, Kelly Betteron, Natasha Marrus, Michael P. Harms, Casy Babb, Tomoyuki, Deanna Barch, JAMA, 2013.

R 4-16 How Children Succeed, Paul Tough, Houghton Mifflin Harcourt, 2012.

R 4-17 Linking Childhood Trauma to long-term Health and Social Consequences, Control [CDC] and Kaiser Permanente [HMO].

R 4-18 Chronic Stress Puts Your Health at Risk, Mayo Clinic Staff, July 8, 2012.

R 4-19 Psychology Today, Public Enemy Number One, July 9, 2007.

R 4-20 Poverty & Despair vs. Education & Opportunity, Al Colella and Joseph H. Crowley, Stillwater River Publications, 2016.

Chapter 5: Poverty in the Classroom: Family & Community Impact

R 5-1 A Framework for Understanding Poverty, 4th Revised Edition, Ruby K. Payne, PhD, aha Process, Inc. 2005.

R 5-2 Poverty & Despair versus Education & Opportunity, Breaking Down the Barriers & Building Bridges, Al Colella, Joseph H. Crowley, Stillwater River Publications, 2016.

R 5-3 Freedom Is Not Enough, The Moynihan Report and America's Struggle over Black Family Life from LBJ to Obama, James T. Patterson, Basic Books, A Member of the Perseus Books Group, 2010.

R 5-4 The Negro Family: The Case for National Action, Daniel Patrick Moynihan.

R 5-5 John Hopkins University, Department of Sociology-related research efforts, Karl Alexander for 25 years, 1981-2010.

R 5-6 How poverty Impacts Education, Bailey Gerber, Forgotten Children Worldwide, March 19, 2020.

R 5-7 Education & Socioeconomic Fact Sheet, The American C

R 5-8 The Rich and the Rest of Us, A Poverty Manifesto, Tavis Smiley and Cornel West, Smiley Books, 2012.

R 5-9 Poverty & Despair versus Education & Opportunity, Al Colella and Joseph H. Crowley, Stillwater River Publications, 2016.

R 5-10 Meet the Press, NBC, May 31, 2020.

R 5-11 Poverty, Not Schools, To Blame For Low Scores, Joseph H. Crowley, Commentary, Providence Journal, November 27, 2015.

R 5-12 'No Excuses', Joseph H. Crowley, Editorial, Providence Journal, December 2, 2015.

R 5-13 Models for School Reforms, Joseph H. Crowley, Providence Journal, August 2, 2019.

R 5-14 Poverty, not bad teachers, is what plagues our schools, Daniel Akst, Newday, August 26, 2012.

R 5-15 Let's Start with the Children, Journey to St. Ann's, A.M. Colella with Steven Lippincott, Westbow Press, 2013.

Chapter 6: Classroom Environment

R 6-1: 'Connect the dots': Definition & Meaning, Merriam-Webster Dictionary, Merriam Web, https://www.Merriam-Webster.com/dictionary/connect-the dots.

R 6-2 What does the phrase "connecting the dots" mean in academc reading terms? Quoran.

R 6-3 https://idioms.thefreedictionary.com/connect the dots.

Chapter 7: Classroom Management & Teacher Leadership

R 7-1 'These Kids Are Out of Control": Why We Must Re-imagine "Classroom Management for Equity 1st Edition, Richard Milner,

Heather B. (Bossert} Cunningham, Lori Delale-O'Connor, Erika Gold Kristenberg, Corwin, 2016.

R 7-2 Classroom Management, Wikipedia.

R 7-3 Solving Discipline Problems, Wolfgang, Charles H. Glickman, Carl D.,1986., ISBN 978-0205086306.

R 7-4 Students Achieving Given Learning Requirements and Goals, Schelli, Alizadeh, Murphy, Bajestani, Ferguson and Dreikurs, [2015]; also, Teachers as Leaders: The Impact of Adler-Dreikus, The Journal of Individual Psychology, January 13, 2012.

R 7-5 Bringing Reality to Classroom Management in Teacher Education, Gordon, Eisenman, S. Edwards, Carey Anne Cushman, Anne Cushman, The Professional Educator, George Regents University, April 1, 2015.

R 7-6 Success Strategies of Inner-City Teachers, A year long study, Moskowitz, Hayman, Jr., J.L., Journal of Educational Research, 69{8}, pp. 283-289, 1976.

R 7-7 Effective Classroom Management and Instruction: A Knowledge Base for Consultation, Berliner, D.C., 1988.

R 7-8 Alternative Educational Systems: Enhancing Instructional Options for All Students, J.L. Gordon, J.E. Zins, M.J. Curtis, Editors, Washington, DC, National Association of School Psychologists, 1988.

R 7-9 Teacher Behavior and Student Achievement, Handbook of Research on Teaching, J.E. Brophy, T.L. Good, M.C. Wittrock, Editor, Macmillan, 1986

R-10 Classroom Management, Students' Perspectives, Goals, and Strategies, Allen, J.D. American Educational Research Journal 23, 1986.

R-11 "These kids are out of control: Why We must re-imagine Classroom Management for Equity", R. Milner, H. Richard IV, Cunningham, B., O'Connor, D., Kestenberg, Erika Gold, ebook, Corwin, August 18, 2018.

R 7-12 Commentary [R 7-11], Andrew Kwok, Assistant Professor, College of Education, February 7, 2018.

R 7-13 Commentary [R7-11], Eric Toshalls, Research Director, February 20, 2018.

R 7-14 Commentary [R 7-11], Carolyn M. Evertson, PhD, Professor of Education, February 2, 2018.

R 7-15 Small Victories, The Rear World of a Teacher, Her Students and their High School, Samuel G. Freedman, Harper & Row Publishers, 1990.

R 7-16 https://www.education.gov.gy/web/index.php/tteachers/tips forteaching/item/1735-seven-key-elements-for effective classroom management.

7-17 Elements of Teaching and Teacher Leadership, James M. Banner, Jr., Harold C. Cannon, Yale University, 1997.

7-18 See R 7-16].

7-19 Understanding Teacher Shortages: 2028 Update, Learning policy Institute, A State-by-State Analysis of the factors Influencing Teacher Supply, Demand and Equity, August 24, 2018.

7-20 Are Teacher Shortages Worse Than We Thought! Education Week, 2019.

7-21 The Teacher Shortage Is Real, Large and Growing and Worse Than We Thought, Economic Policy Institute, Emma Garcia, Elaine Weiss, March 26, 2019.

Additional Relevant References

7-22 The teachers who changed my life, Felicia Nimue Ackerman, MY TURN, Providence Journal, April 26, 2016.

7-23 It Won't Be Easy: An exceedingly Honest [and Slightly Unprofessional Love Letter to Teaching], T. Rademacher, University of Minnesota Press, April 25, 2017.

7-24 The Elements of Teaching, James M. Banner and Harold C. Cannon, ISBH 030006929-4, Yale University, 1997.

R 7-25 Accelerating Per Coaching of Teacher Leadership for Profession

Inquiry, Charteris and Smardon, International Journal of Mentoring and Coaching in Education, 108, April, 2014.

R 7-26 The San Miguel School, Providence RI [Director: John Wolf].

R 7-27 Inspiring Minds, inspiringminds.org.

7-28 Educational Forum, A. Lieberman and L. Miller, Educational Forum, p. 155, 2005.

7-29 Poverty & Despair versus Education & Opportunity, Breaking Down Barriers & Building Bridges, A. Colella, Joseph H. Crowley, Stillwater River Publications, 2016.

7-30 Teacher Leadership Skills, Framework, 2009.

7-31 https://azquotes.com/author/20944-Linda-Darling-Hammond, Retrieval, February, 2021.

7-32 Leadership and the New Science, Margaret J. Wheatley, Barrett Kohler Publisher, January 15, 2001.

7-33 Ten Roles for Teacher Leadership, Cindy Harrison and Joellen Killion, ASCD, September 1, 2007.

7-34 Taking the Lead: New Roles for Teachers and School-based Coach{s}, J. Killion and C. Harrison 2nd Edition, Leaning Forward-The Professional Learning Association, January 1, 2017.

R 7-35 Scholarly Articles for Teacher Leadership Skills, Rebecca Cheung, Thomas Reinhart, Elisa Stone..., PDK International, Phi Delts Kappan [PDK], October 20, 2020.

7-36 The First Year Teacher's Guide to preparing for the School Year, June 17, 2019.

7-37 New Teacher Center, newteachercenter.org.

7-38 Teacher: A One-size Fits All Approach to Education is Stifling, https://www.washingtonpost.com.

7-39 R.I.'s Chance to Remake Schools, *OPINION*, Journal, April 18, 2015.

7-40 Teachers as Leaders, Ann Lieberman and Lynne Miller, The Educational Forum 69, June, 2005.

7-41 Teacher Leadership: A systemic review, methodological quality assessment and conceptual framework, C. Scott, H. van Roekel, L. Tummers, Educational Research Review, 2020.

7-42 Classroom Management for Elementary Teachers, 11th Edition, Carolyn M. Evertson, Edmund T. Emmer, Inge Poole, Pearson, May 22, 2021.

Chapter 8: Systemic/Functional/Inclusive Model: Linkage & Dynamics

R 8-1 Revisiting the Infamous Hawthorne Effect, Peter Budnick, PhD, https://ergoweb.com/revisiting-the-infamous-hawthorne-effect/ CPE, November 7, 2012.

R 8-2 The Light in the Heart: Inspirational Thoughts for Living Your Best Life, Kindle Edition, Roy T. Bennett.

Chapter 9: Roles and Values of Advocacy, Support & Mentoring for the Teachers in the Classrooms…and Their Students…and Their Families

R 9-1 Let's Start with the Children, Colella, A. Lippincott S., Westbow Press, 2013.

R 9-2 Poverty, Not Schools, To Blame for Low Scores, Joseph H. Crowley, *OPINION,* Providence Journal, 2013.

R 9-3 Mentoring Definition, What is A Mentor…Google Search.

R 9-4 35 Questions Mentors Should Ask Their Mentees/Together Mentoring Software, https://www..togetherplatform.com/blog/questions-to-ask-a-mentee.

R 9-5 Web-based Mentoring Software…Google Search.

R 9-6 Mentoring in The Classsroom, https://bartleby.com/essay/Mentoring-in-the-Classroom-FJ7WUUF923M.

R 9-7 Learning Readiness, EARLY LITERACY NETWORK I DEANS FOR IMPACT.

R 9-8 Test Scores Show Kids Not Erasing Pandemic Losses, Heather Hollingworth and Carolyn Thompson, Associated Press, Providence Journal, July 12, 2023.

R 9-9 Foster Kids are falling further academically, *YOUR TURN,* Rep. Julie A. Casimiro, Providence Journal, June 4 2023.

R 9-10 Child Literacy Programs in America, Beginners Thru 6th Grade: After School and Summer. Literacy Programs Feature A Curriculum Built Around the Literacy Block. Also, Innovative Approaches to Literacy [IAL]; IAL supports high quality programs to develop literacy skills brom birth to the 12th grade.

Some Relevant 'Quick-Read' References Across All Chapters

R 9-11 How Children Succeed, Paul Tough, Houghton Mifflin Harcourt, 2012

R 9-12 R.I.'s Chance to Remake Schools, Ron Wolk, *OPINION,* Providence Journal, April 28, 2015.

R 9-13 Poverty & Despair versus Education & Opportunity, Joseph H. Crowley, Al Colella, Stillwater River Publications, 2016.

R 9-14 The Elements of Teaching, James C. Banner, Harold C. Cannon, Yale University, 1997.

R 9-15 Small Victories, Samuel G. Freedman, Harper Perrenial, 1991.

R 9-16 And Still We Rise, Miles Corwin, Harper Perrenial, 2000.

R 9-17 Among School Children, Tracy Kidde, Harper Perrenial, 2001.

R 9-18 Five Tips For Effective Mentoring, Marina Picciotto, The New Academy of Sciences

R 9-19 Mentor Guide, Association for Computing Machinery/SIGUCCS, [ACM]

R 9-20 Introducing the 2020 National Mentoring Summit Presenting Exhibitor: Innovative Mentoring Software.

R 9-21 Juvenile Mentoring Program [JUMP]: Federally Funded Juvenile Justice & Delinquency Prevention [JJDP].

R 9-22 A Systemic Assessment of the Evidence, David L. Dubois, Nelson Portillo, Jean E. Rhodes, Naida Silverthorn and Jeffrey C. Valentine, Association of Psychological Science [APS], October 20, 2011.

Chapter 10: Costs of Poverty

R 10-1 Poverty, not schools, to blame for low scores, Joseph H. Crowley, *OPINION,* Providence Journal, November 27, 2015.

R 10-2The Road out of Poverty still runs past the schoolhouse door, Drew Snyder, https://twitter.com.

R 10-3 Poverty & Despair versus Education & Opportunity, Breaking Down the Barriers Building Bridges, Al Colella and Joseph H. Crowley, Stillwater River Publications, 2016.

R 10-4 https://www.poverty-inequalities.com

R 10-5 Dana Mitra, Associate Professor Maya Angelou.

R 10-6 Edutopia, January 4, 2019.

R 10-7 National Institute for Early Institute Research.

R 10-8 U.S. Department of Justice [pre-K classes].

R 10-9 America's Promise Alliance.

R 10-10 Social Benefits of Public Education, Dana Mitra, Associate Professor of Education, Penn State University.

R 10-11 Don't just spend the money, *invest* in R.I.s children, Joseph H. Crowley, *COMMENTARY,* Providence Journal, January 5, 2022.

Some Closing Thoughts

When written in Chinese, the 'word' crisis is composed or two characters. One represents danger and the other represents opportunity.

—JOHN F. KENNEDY

Success is liking yourself, liking what you do and liking how you do it.

—MAYA ANGELOU

To teach is to learn twice.

—JOSEPH JOUBERT

The reasonable thing is to learn from those who can teach.

—ANTIGONE BY SOPHOCLES

I want to understand myself, to understand others, I want to be all that I am capable of...

— KATHERINE MANSFIELD [JOURNAL]

A journey of a thousand miles must begin with a single step.

—THE WAY OF LAO TZU

Education is the key to unlock the golden door of freedom.

—GEORGE WASHINGTON CARVER

The beautiful thing about learning is that no one can take it away from you.

—B. B. KING

A teacher affects eternity she/he can never tell where her/his influence stops.

—UNKNOWN

The roots of education are bitter but the fruit is steep.

—ARISTOTLE

He who opens a prison door, closes a prison.

—ALBERT EINSTEIN

Education is the most powerful weapon which you can use to change the world.

—NELSON MANDELA

The beginning of one's education does start with the family, continues within the classrooms but also in the classroom of life.

About the Authors

Al Colella, PhD

Date: August 25, 2015

He is a 1951 honor graduate from St. Raphael Academy in Pawtucket, RI, and recipient of the Latin Medal there; he also played football for the 'Saints' earning Class A honors several times. He was also the recipient of a football scholarship to Rutgers University. While at Rutgers, he was drafted and is a U.S. Army veteran and a graduate of the Army's Leadership School. He received his BS Degree in Electrical Engineering from the University of Rhode Island in 1961 and translated mathematical papers from French to English as part of his work-study program there. He also served as a mentor and tutor for his fellow students in several courses at URI but is better and humorously remembered for tutoring students in their challenging statistics class , all of whom received a grade of 'A' while he earned a 'B.' He entered government service at the United States Naval Underwater Ordnance Station at Newport, RI, pursuing graduate studies at the University of Rhode Island while working as a full-time Instrumentation Engineer and raising a family. He was awarded an MS Degree in Electrical Engineering [Control Systems] in 1965 and a Ph.D. in Electrical Engineering [Nonlinear Adaptive Control Systems in 1973] from the University of Rhode Island.

In 1964, he took the position of Technical Assistant to the Laboratory Director for Control and Information Systems at NASA's Electronic Research Center. He was then appointed Technical Advisor to the Deputy Director of the Deep Submergence Rescue Vehicle [DSRV] Program at MIT's Draper Laboratory in 1966. Program responsibility included technical program reviews and the assessment of guidance, control and display systems, laboratory real-time [man-in-the-loop], and computer simulations. He also served as a Guidance & Control Engineer with Raytheon's Missile Systems Division. In 1970, Dr. Colella served as the Technical Assistant to various program managers at the Transportation Systems Center of the United States Department of Transportation. In 1978, he returned to the United States Naval Undersea Warfare Center until his retirement in 1993 after 33 years of government service. This most recent assignment [lasting 25 years] involved the mathematical modeling of complex systems, expert system development, and communications systems [where he teamed with members of the United States submarine fleet in the analysis of tactical communications]. In 1989, he served as Technical assistant to the Associate Director for Research and Technology. He was responsible for the conception, analysis, and development of emerging technology assessment methodologies. He also served as Program Manager for the Center's Industrial Research & Development Program.

Upon his retirement in October of 1993, Dr. Colella was awarded membership in the 'Order of the Decibel' for his outstanding contributions and dedication in the areas of artificial intelligence and the mentoring of the Center's new professionals, and providing leadership in the Center's Industrial Research & Development Program. In particular, for his organization and management of the Center's IR&D Symposium with industry that became a model for the future of government and industrial interactions. It is important to note that this particular award is made selectively to retiring staff members who have contributed broadly and significantly to advancing the overall performance of the Center's mission.

Upon his retirement from government service, Dr. Colella extended his 30 years of teaching and mentoring within the government and, more formally, in both undergraduate and graduate programs [at various colleges and universities] and, then, by joining the faculty at the School of Technology at Johnson & Wales University. His areas of teaching there included all levels of mathematics, communications, robotics, artificial intelligence, instrumentation, control systems, systems analysis, modeling, and simulation. His classes gave equal attention and emphasis to those skills needed to be successful in a specific technological area but, more importantly, to those skills [he always referred to them as the 'keys of life' that are needed to 'open doors' of opportunity] required for life success as an individual. In 1995, he was appointed as Head of the School of Technology and became the prime facilitator for upgrading all technology curricula and programs. He was the principal advocate and mover for the integration of relevant areas of technology into *all academic programs* at the University.

During his 43 years of professional service, he became a mentor, advocate, facilitator, friend, confidant, and, more often than not, a father figure to myriad students and even some of the faculty. He always considered this particular role—family, community, government, and military service—the most formative, meaningful, and rewarding phase of his life. Whatever the arena, Dr. Colella always found a way [often creatively] to 'make a difference.' Once asked "Why?" about these roles, he simply replied, "Other people—some unknown to me—made a difference within my lifetime, so why not 'pass it on' [aka 'paying it forward']." He was a walking and talking reminder that "Each of us really stands on the shoulders of others!" and "From those to whom much is given, much is expected!"

He has authored/co-authored more than 50 papers, articles, books, and reports in his expertise and experienced areas of technology and management. He presented papers at a number of professional conferences where he sometimes received the 'best paper' award.

In parallel with his 43 years of professional activity, he was quite active in outreach and community service to those in need and, most importantly, being an advocate and mentor for his family, children, and his 15 grandchildren. Some of these activities beyond the family included Big Brothers, advocating for teens within his faith community, Literacy Volunteers of America [LVA], Random Acts of Kindness, fund raising for families in need, home repair ministry, and being an active supporter of Saint Raphael Academy where he served as a scout for its football teams and was a founder of the Saints Club—an organization that was very much an advocate of the athletic programs in the 50s, 60s, and 70s. This latter activity was fueled by his awareness and appreciation that his years at Saint Raphael Academy were most formative for him. His outreach and community service activities were many, and each challenging, but he always saw them as opportunities!

Additionally, he was the initiator, motivator, and facilitator of efforts to address the needs of those in poverty and despair. His book with Steven Lippincott, *Let's Start with the Children* [published in 2013], relates the heart-breaking but also heart-warming and inspirational events of a 15-year ministry with the children and families of the challenging environment of the South Bronx in New York City. This ministry was the inspiration for *Let's Start with the Children,* which, in turn, became the inspirational force enabling the writing [with co-author Joseph H. Crowley] and the publication of *Poverty & Despair versus Education & Opportunity.*

Joseph H. Crowley

Joe Crowley has lived the life. He grew up in a housing project, the oldest of nine siblings whose father was an alcoholic and whose mother, who was a saint, was overstressed in managing a home and nine children with little help from his father. His father worked as a fireman, which involved more than seventy hours per week in the fire station, but he would then spend his off days and evenings in a bar very often over the years. He is thankful an aunt and uncle took an interest in him, and today, he understands the benefits of having caring adults in one's life.

Not having much parental supervision, he was able to leave high school without a diploma. Fortunately, he was able to join the U.S. Air Force. A combination of maturation and being given considerable responsibility while in the service led to his desire for a college degree. His first ambition was to be a history teacher, but with his less -than-stellar high school record, getting into a four-year college was out of the question.

Having been exposed to computers while in the Air Force, this was early on in the use of computers, and becoming a computer programmer looked like a good path. He was accepted into what was then Johnson & Wales Junior College—on probation because of his high school record. Older and wiser, he graduated second in his class—in high school, he had been in the bottom five.

Within a year of beginning a c omputer programmer/analyst career, Joe had the opportunity to teach programming in a public career and technical high school. This led to more education where, within five years while teaching, he was able to earn a baccalaureate degree with high honors and an MBA at the University of Rhode Island—being elected to two national honor societies.

He sees his transition from lacking a high school diploma to an MBA as reflecting the potential that might well be lost as children growing up in poverty environments try to overcome the barriers and find the bridges to work their way out. Inner- city schools are loaded with Joes who might or might not break the bonds of poverty.

Over his career, Joe has served as a teacher, assistant principal, principal, school district business manager, and, for a time, as an interim superintendent of schools. He has served as president of the Rhode Island Association of School Principals, president of the Massachusetts Association of School Business Managers, and chair of the New England Association of Schools and Colleges Commission on Technical and Career Institutions. He is the past executive director of the

Rhode Island Association of School Principals, serving on a number of education-related boards and committees.

Joe has been advocating for children living in poverty and school safety for many years, having published a number of commentaries in local newspapers. His main point is that learning differences between more and less affluent children result from their homes—not their schools. Our schools are not failing.

He and his wife Kathryn, a retired superintendent of schools, live in Cranston, RI, and enjoy the four children and eight grandchildren they share.

Kimberly Deninger

Kimberly has taught in public school systems for nine years (as of 2023). Her experience includes elementary education, special education for individuals with mild to moderate disabilities, and teaching English language learners. Kim began by graduating from Flagler College in 2014 with bachelor's degrees in elementary and special education with additional endorsements in English language learning and reading. Wanting to remain in warm Florida weather, Kim began in the one job that would hire a fresh college graduate at a charter school in northern Florida. In those years, Kim discovered that it was a struggle to establish sufficient classroom support for her students, most importantly, those with learning differences! From those challenges with sufficient resources, she decided to pursue greater understanding in the area of curriculum and the potential impact on students with learning differences. She enrolled and later graduated from George Washington University in 2018 with a Master's degree in Curriculum and Instruction, with additional accreditation in Autism Spectrum Disorder. After graduation, Kim stayed in the DC-Virginia area to teach and serve her local school communities. After teaching in a dual special education classroom (resource & self-contained), Kim found that she again had a lack of resources to serve those children with the highest needs. Though the pandemic paused her continued education, in 2022, Kim enrolled and is attending Simmons University, where she is studying Behavior Analysis at the time of this writing.

A common theme Kim saw across the schools where she taught was the lack of student learning readiness. Developing learning readiness was not taught in any program she had attended but appeared most critical to individual student success. The transition into an ABA-driven practice holds the intention of supporting and instructing learners to develop both learning readiness as well as school readiness.

Passionate about her students, Kim continues to strive to improve teaching practices for relevant and accessible learning for all students.

www.ingramcontent.com/pod-product-compliance
Ingram Content Group UK Ltd.
Pitfield, Milton Keynes, MK11 3LW, UK
UKHW060116010826
14089UKWH00003B/15

9 781963 296099